ENGAGED

Creating a Great Organization through Extraordinary Employee and User Engagement

Praise for ENGAGED

"*Engaged* is a fantastic book that every company leader and CEO should read if they are concerned about increasing the engagement of their associates. The stories and examples are great highlights to bring home the key components of the book. Jason is a great champion for associate engagement and user-designed solutions."

Timothy Doss, Divisional VP, Enterprise Transformation Kindred Healthcare

"After working with and knowing Jason for over a decade and benefiting from *Idealized Design* which he and Dr. Russell Ackoff authored, it is remarkable to have read *Engaged* and learn the next chapter in creating value by harnessing organizational and individual engagement. I will definitely use the wisdom and concepts provided in this book and highly recommend to others."

Brian Bules, Global Head of Talent Solutions, GlaxoSmithKline

"*Engaged* is an excellent book, especially for leaders who are looking for a practical and elegant way to achieve greater impact in their organizations and win both the hearts and the minds of their employees. Jason combines the wisdom of some great thought leaders with research and integrates it with his own extensive experience. He shows how we can make our organizations come to life by providing meaning and purpose for both leaders and employees at every level. A great read!"

Stephen Hart, Vice President, Human Resources Federal Reserve Bank of Philadelphia

"Jason Magidson shows us the practical yet powerful path to improving engagement and performance in his latest book, *Engaged: Creating a Great Organization through Extraordinary Employee and User Engagement.* As technology continues to move faster and more generations are present in the workforce, Jason conveys with stories and charm how to move the dial on results through engagement."

David Henkin, Corporate Executive, Author, Adjunct Faculty, Villanova University

"*Engaged* provides practical customer-oriented techniques to improve employee effectiveness, performance and development. Jason includes many real world examples demonstrating the superior results - I highly recommend."

Joe Meier
Former SVP Global Procurement, GlaxoSmithKline

"Making the connection between happy employees and lasting customer relationships is gaining importance as today's workforce seeks increased meaning in their work life. *Engaged* provides actionable, proven solutions that drive the positive change businesses need and employees desire."

Geoff Edwards, SVP, Market Operations, Fedbid

"The practices found in Jason's terrific book, *Engaged*, will enable your organization to realize its full potential by living the truth that your people are everything rather than just saying it."
Mark D Steele, Author of Projects On Purpose

Dedication

In memoriam to Russell Ackoff, Sheldon Rovin, and Herman Wrice, and in appreciation to Jamshid Gharajedaghi – generous mentors all.

VI ENGAGED

....

Acknowledgements

We thank the following people who helped make this book possible: Rob Weker and Pam Magidson for reviewing the manuscript and providing insightful suggestions; Ronnette Watson for her interview, which forms a chapter; Linda Amoroso and Mark Steele for their encouragement during the writing process; Kathie Beans for professional editing; Linda Galvin for professional cover design and book layout; And, last but not least, Julia Magidson for illustration.

VIII   ENGAGED

Table of Contents

Foreword

When asked about their most important asset, most corporate leaders instinctively respond, "It's our people." But is it really? When employees are asked if they believe they are the most valuable asset, their responses range from loud laughter to acute nausea to pure anger.

After working in and around corporations for over 40 years, I've found that the company with truly energized and highly engaged workers is rare. Furthermore, many executives are not aware of the extent of the dissatisfaction that impacts the bottom line. *ENGAGED: Creating a Great Organization through Extraordinary Employee and User Engagement* is the answer to this age-old dilemma.

When I first met Jason Magidson at a well-known Philadelphia tavern almost 20 years ago, I had been newly appointed to lead a global procurement support group. The group badly needed a cultural upgrade and "new ways of working." The current thinking was that the support group (the experts) was all knowing and would tell procurement users how they should do their work. This approach created much ill will. ("The users are too stupid to follow our processes.") It was obvious I needed to create a new environment that focused on user satisfaction and getting results. I was mulling the issue with a close work associate who said, "I know a guy who's a little different, but he might be just what you need." Well, in that initial meeting with Jason Magidson, it took me about 10 minutes to recognize that I needed him to help drive the necessary change. A few months later he became part of my team.

Thus began an almost two-decade working relationship in which I've been part of groups or watched groups of employees use the various techniques described in this book. I've witnessed "MAG-nificent" results over and over again in a variety of situations and organizations. Jason's techniques have provided breakthrough results for organizations trying to improve products, services, internal systems and processes and even the organizations themselves. Employee satisfaction came along with the breakthrough results as countless disengaged employees became truly engaged.

Now, I believe in big aspirations – delivering step-change results that drive benefit to the bottom line. During our 10 years together at pharmaceutical giant GlaxoSmithKline, Jason and I did just that. We used many of the techniques described in this book to create user-built systems and processes. As a result of our efforts, GlaxoSmithKline was recognized internationally for its world class electronic procurement platform. The company's annual investment in the platform is returned in incremental savings every three working days.

Whether you are leading a company, an organization or are just part of a team, you can use this book to begin generating excitement, deliver significant results through user design, and begin a new culture that people will want to be part of.

Jason shared the manuscript draft with me during production and I gave the "top 10 list poll" (found in the introduction and designed to measure employee engagement) to a number of employees at the large corporation where I was working.   Laughter filled the halls as employees answered the questions and determined they were disengaged and even actively disengaged.   This same company had posters all over the walls about what a great place to work it was.   Again, it's that perception gap I mentioned earlier. It exists in most organizations.

Some of my favorite chapters include: Involving Employees and Users in Design, Work Backwards from Where You Want to Be, De-emphasize Internally Focused Metrics and Quotas, Be More of a Giver Than a Taker, Create Visions, and Listen to Your Employees.

Regardless of where you are in the company hierarchy, this book will help you make a real difference.   Personally, I never found satisfaction in doing things in a small way.   I also never found satisfaction in competing with other employees.   As I learned to think like Jason Magidson I found it very interesting that you can do big things even if you are starting from a small space, and you can be hugely successful by adopting a user design that encompasses everyone's ideas and everyone wins as a team.

Think big. Use this book to your advantage to achieve results you would have never thought possible.   Jason Magidson has been putting these practices to work, learning by doing and improving through others' ideas and contributions for more than 30 years. The book represents the culmination of his efforts.

In my 40-plus years of working, I've had many experiences and known many people, but I've never known anyone quite like Jason.   He is the embodiment of this book and puts its wisdom into practice every day.

This is a must-read for anyone who desires to make a real difference in their organization. And it's a must-read for every employee who wants to develop into a true leader.

Corporations today are at a crossroads, the intersection of people and technology. We will always need both, so shouldn't we focus on operating in a way that elicits actively engaged employees? There's never been a better time to start the process than TODAY!

R. Gregg Brandyberry
Supply Chain Management Educator

Introduction

In his lectures, Mark Twain would occasionally quote his friend, Charles Dudley Warner: "Everyone talks about the weather, but nobody does anything about it." It's much the same with employee engagement at most organizations. Companies do their annual or biannual surveys, but engagement levels remain disappointing in most. Extraordinary engagement is rare despite efforts to improve it. Too many people derive little joy at work, and they count down the days, hours, and minutes until the end of the work week.

Much has been written about the relationship between employee engagement and business performance, but much less has been written about specific actions to improve it. That's where this book comes in. It offers a diverse mix of practical, proven actions you can take to enhance employee and user engagement. You can mix and match and use the actions that best fit you and your organization. You may not agree with everything recommended here, and that's okay.

Highly engaged employees are the foundation of great organizations, and the aim of this book is to help people create great organizations where:

- People are excited about their work.
- The work enables employees to flourish while bringing meaning to their lives.
- Employees have a chance to shape and deliver on the organization's goals.
- The organization's products or services satisfy *and* delight their customers.

Greatness requires many components. This book draws on our 30 years of personal professional experience as well as on research and ideas from other writers. No one book or method has all of the answers, so we offer our perspective, and we also point you to other notable research and writings.

Although I am the author of this book, I write from the "we" perspective because many of the examples I use are taken from different engagements involving multiple people. We try to keep the book interesting (and, at times, humorous) by telling you stories that are either from our personal experience or examples from great practices at other organizations.

So, let's jump in with a humorous story: An awkward incident occurred when we were preparing to facilitate a process improvement session for an Aquafresh toothpaste factory. It was going to be a long session, so we made sure to hit the restroom before we started. Three men were in there, and we overheard one of them complaining to his colleagues that he had to go to some bull$#!+ four-hour meeting with someone from Corporate. We chuckled, but didn't say anything as we walked out together and into the meeting room. We enjoyed the reaction on his face when he realized that we were "the guys from Corporate." The story has a happy ending, however, and this man was delighted with the session outcome.

Our session focused on designing the ideal maintenance, repair, and operations (MRO) process for the toothpaste manufacturing line. We told the 25 participants to pretend that their MRO process had been destroyed last night and they now had the opportunity to design their ideal process from scratch. As we got into the session, the group quickly became liberated and engaged. They came up with many good ideas and the excitement in the room was palpable. One idea is illustrative. The team said that it would ideally like to be able to spend money on repairs -- up to a certain dollar amount -- without having to get plant manager approval. The team explained that waiting for approvals led to significant lost production due to line downtime. At the end of the session, we asked the plant manager to join us and review the proposals. When the group explained to him that approval delays were resulting in lost production, he immediately granted them standing approval to spend up to $500 on any repair. At the end of the meeting, the man we had overheard in the restroom came up to us, shook our hands and thanked us. The participants were energized, optimistic, and bought into the planned next steps.

It was a great feeling to see this man go from actively disengaged to highly engaged in just four hours. And we'll tell you a secret: We were fairly confident that this would happen, but you'll have to read further to learn how we achieved it.

To emphasize why we feel engagement is so important to happiness and success, we ask you to think back to some point in your career (it may even be now) when you felt powerless, disengaged, or even alienated. We wouldn't be surprised if one of the following was occurring:

- Management had little interest in hearing what you think.
- You felt like you were a passenger in the back seat who knew where you needed to go, but the driver was not listening.
- You were given little or no latitude in how to do your job.
- You were faced with quotas or arbitrary and strict deadlines that resulted in poor quality
- You believed you weren't able to make an impact.
- Your contributions weren't being properly recognized.
- You were constantly being told that you are doing things wrong.
- A manager was creating an environment of fear.

We've all worked for bosses who created a negative culture. For more than one of them, we became delighted whenever we learned that they would unexpectedly be away from the office.

Year after year, the Gallup Organization conducts a poll of employee engagement[1] around the world, and the news isn't encouraging. Some recent findings:

- Only 13% of employees are engaged at work(!!!), with engagement defined as "psychologically committed to their jobs and likely to be making positive contributions to their organizations." So, if only one in

---

[1] Gallup. "Worldwide, 13% of Employees Are Engaged at Work." October 28, 2013. Web URL: http://www.gallup.com/poll/165269/worldwide-employees-engaged-work.aspx

eight employees *is* engaged, it's disturbing to think about how the others are feeling and what they may be doing.

- The 63% who are not engaged "lack motivation and are less likely to invest discretionary effort in organizational goals or outcomes." However, we know from ample research that people don't lack motivation – humans are intrinsically motivated. If employees are not engaged, factors in their organizations are likely hindering their ability to actualize their motivations. We'll talk more later about how to support motivation.
- The other 24% of employees are "actively disengaged," which Gallup defines as "unhappy and unproductive at work and liable to spread negativity to coworkers." Gallup concludes, "… low levels of engagement among global workers continue to hinder gains in economic productivity and life quality in much of the world," and we agree. However, we're optimistic because we personally know organizations where the overwhelming majority of employees are engaged, and we will share what those organizations are doing to obtain that level of engagement.

Gallup's engagement rates are somewhat better in the United States, but they're still dismal. 69.7% are either not engaged or actively disengaged. Amazingly, only three in 10 are engaged! It's interesting to note that high rates of disengagement are not pooled among those with less education. A slightly lower percentage of those with postgraduate work or a degree are engaged (30.3%) than those with a high school diploma or less (32.7%). Two thirds of highly educated people are disengaged!

But enough with the statistics. We now turn to our own unscientific top 10 list poll to see how engaged *you* are at your workplace. Simply answer true or false to the following statements:

1. As I start the new work week, I often feel stressed or depressed.
2. As Friday approaches, my mood elevates.
3. When I find out that the boss cancelled a meeting or is away from the office, I feel joy.
4. In most meetings my ideas are either shut down or I decline to offer them.
5. I frequently fantasize about how much nicer things will be when I can retire.
6. When I am off work, I rarely get excited when I think about the coming work week.
7. I'm rarely praised, and I worry that I could lose my job at any time.
8. The culture is about finger pointing rather than partnering for success.
9. Our company, project, or group is headed in the wrong direction, but speaking up is risky.
10. People usually aren't smiling.

Count one point for each "True," and add them up. If you scored six or more, there's a good chance you are disengaged.

It will not come as a surprise that studies link engagement to a company's performance. Gallup did another meta-analysis of research on the relationship between employee engagement and business performance outcomes.[2] This analysis, covering 1.4 million employees, demonstrates strong correlations between employee engagement and key performance outcomes (across industries and regions of the world) including:

- Customer ratings
- Profitability
- Productivity
- Employee turnover
- Safety incidents
- Absenteeism
- Quality (defects)

Here's what Gallup found:

> *"Work units in the top quartile in employee engagement outperformed bottom-quartile units by 10% on customer ratings, 22% in profitability, and 21% in productivity. Work units in the top quartile also saw significantly lower turnover (25%) ... shrinkage (28%), and absenteeism (37%) and fewer safety incidents (48%) ... and quality defects (41%)."*

The Gallup study is a correlation analysis, which demonstrates that employee engagement is strongly related to these performance metrics, but it doesn't demonstrate causality. In other words, it doesn't show whether employee engagement causes better performance, whether better

---

[2] http://www.gallup.com/businessjournal/163130/employee-engagement-drives-growth.aspx

performance causes higher employee engagement, or whether they both cause each other to go up and/or down. However, while causal analyses are generally far rarer than correlational analyses, recent research published in the *Journal of Occupational and Organizational Psychology* by researchers at the University of Zurich, Switzerland, and University of Saarlandes, Germany, suggests that the effect of employee engagement on organizational performance is longer lasting than the effect of organizational performance on employee engagement:[3]

> *We contrasted both temporal directions within a data set of 755 employees from the retail banking division of a large bank, nested in 34 business units, for the period of 2005–2008, allowing for a controlled environment and consistent data capturing over time. We studied the relationship of organizational commitment aggregated to the business unit level with two business unit performance indicators (financial achievement and customer satisfaction).*

> - *Our study suggests a potential answer to the chicken-and-egg problem (i.e., the temporal ordering of the job attitude–job performance relationship): Our theory and data suggest that the influence of performance on subsequent attitudes might be less persistent over time than vice versa.*

---

[3] http://onlinelibrary.wiley.com/doi/10.1111/j.2044-8325.2012.02054.x/abstract

- *Our study sheds new light onto which timely dimensions are involved in the job attitude–job performance relationship: While the impact of performance on attitudes diminishes after 1 year, the impact of attitudes on performance lasts up to 3 years.*

The authors conclude:

Results indicated that organizational commitment had a more persistent influence on performance at the business unit level than vice versa. Consistent with prior research, this suggests that job attitudes may come first, and that practitioners might be well advised to aim to improve job attitudes in order to boost performance.

The good news is that much is known about how to create employee and customer engagement. We believe that the approaches and methods in our book not only indirectly improve business outcomes through better employee engagement, but also directly improve those outcomes through other factors including process improvement, transformation, culture change, and customer focus.

Two organizations illustrate examples of what goes right when employees are engaged: Griffin Hospital and online shoe and apparel retailer Zappos.com. We'll go into more detail later about how Griffin Hospital and Zappos engaged employees, but for now we'll sketch a picture. It's no accident that Zappos' employees are engaged. CEO, Tony Hsieh, has focused intently on creating a culture of collaboration and extraordinary customer service that makes employees proud and excited to work there. For example, associates who receive phone calls from customers are not measured on length of call; they can stay on as long as needed to ensure the customer is happy. Customers are not bounced around just to meet a call length metric. Additionally, associates are empowered to solve many customer problems without having to go to a supervisor for approval. Employees are satisfied that they are doing the right thing and customers are delighted by the ease of doing business with Zappos.

Similarly, Connecticut-based Griffin Hospital's commitment to creating an extraordinary patient experience has inspired and excited employees to put their hearts into their work. Imagine employees who went from putting 40% of their energy into their job to 120%, meaning they are so excited that they are coming up with ideas outside of work that they cannot wait to share with their colleagues. Griffin Hospital was able to create this employee engagement by committing to creating an extraordinary experience for patients and for family members and friends visiting the hospital. Employees participate in initiatives such as making it easy for visitors to park, making it comfortable for family to stay overnight, and creating comfortable waiting areas.

Now let's turn to another true, funny story. We were traveling on business in Heidelberg, Germany, and in the evening partook in our hobby of collecting real-life humorous stories for a book we were writing. We asked our taxi driver if he had any true-life funny stories from experiences with his passengers. After a long pause, he said:

> *One night a drunken man stumbled toward my taxi and asked me how much it would cost to take him home, which was about 15 kilometers away. I told him it would cost 30 euros. He mumbled that the fare was too expensive and that he would drive his own car. I said*

okay and continued on my way, taking a few other passengers to their destinations. About an hour later I got a call from the dispatcher asking me to pick up a passenger from the local police station. When I arrived, I was surprised to see that the passenger was the same man who had refused the ride earlier. I learned that he had crashed his car into a gas station, wrecking his vehicle. Thereafter he was processed for drunk driving. It was with irony that I said, "It's still going to cost you 30 euros.

Trying to implement your ideas without engaging other people and getting their buy-in is a bit like the experience of the drunk driver who went it alone. You're going to experience a lot of pain — we repeat, a lot of pain — and make innocent bystanders suffer. And you're going to pay the price of delays, wasted money, resistance, lost time, damaged relationships, and possibly even losing your job or seriously damaging your company. You might as well get others engaged early on. But, you may ask, "How do we get these folks engaged and bought in? Reading this book will help you identify ways to engage employees. Each chapter discusses a different idea for engaging employees. We hope it helps you make the desired impact.

First, though, we offer this definition of employee engagement:

An employee is engaged in her work when she:
- Is eager for her work week to resume.
- Finds herself thinking outside of work hours about what she could do to make more impact.
- Believes her work is a calling, rather than just a way to make money.

- Is excited that she is part of something bigger than herself.

Part I

Interactive Design

1. Involve Employees and Users in Design

Giving employees the opportunity to shape what they are working on and to help set the direction for their organization is a powerful way to foster engagement. The same is true for involving users of a product, service, or process in its design. Deeply involving internal or external users, such as customers or community constituents, offers significant benefits. Experience has taught us that *how* people are engaged is pivotal in determining whether truly constructive engagement is achieved or whether resistance takes hold. Here's a cartoon that illustrates the point:

We often show this cartoon to people and ask what they think the managers are doing wrong. Many respond that the managers apparently already developed a plan and timeline without consulting others and are simply looking for endorsement of their agenda. Some say that they are acting arrogantly, as if they know better than others what is needed. One can expect that this management plan will probably fail because others won't support it. The outcome will be somewhat like the story about the drunk who drove instead of taking the taxi – a lot of time and money wasted, no resulting improvements, and plunging engagement.

We have observed three types of approaches to designing solutions. (These approaches apply to employees as well as "users;" we say "user" here for short.) The first approach, which the manager in the cartoon has taken, is "design _for_ the users." In some cases, it's a matter of arrogance: "I know better what is needed than those people and I want the chance to be the hero and save the day." In other cases a manager believes that involving others in the process will slow things down or harm the results.

Unfortunately, design-_for_-the-users approach fares poorly because people commit to solutions for which they feel ownership. Without ownership, employees will likely be unenthusiastic or even resistant. It's like parents trying to force their teenagers to do something. How well does that work?

A variation of the design-_for_-the-users approach occurs when one or more executives set an aggressive timeline that forces a project team to cut corners and make assumptions and decisions on behalf of the users. This approach leads to user resistance when the final solution doesn't meet their needs, and it hurts morale because the employees who want to create a great user experience do not get a chance to build what is desired.

A second approach to designing solutions is "design _with_ the users." In this scenario, solution providers obtain high level, rather than detailed, user input. For example, they may conduct an online survey to explore user requirements, or they may meet one-on-one or in small groups and ask questions. If the solution providers hold a brainstorming session, they might collect ideas over a short period and then get little additional input. This is generally followed by designing the solution mostly on their own. Unfortunately, there are several problems with this approach. The most poignant is that when they launch the solution, the users say it does not meet their needs. Obtaining input from users without involving them in the details results in missing nuanced requirements. Even though "design *with* the users" is preferable to "design *for* the users," development can go astray as illustrated in the following classic cartoon from the 1970s.

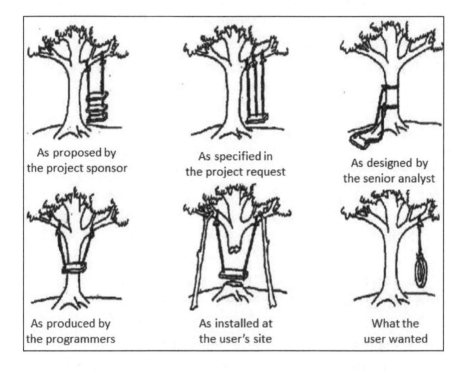

When they believe they used a good process to obtain input, solution providers can become perplexed about why users are not adopting their solution. But there is a more robust method of obtaining input.

A third approach, which we have found to be extraordinarily effective in supportive work environments, is "design _by_ the users." With this approach, users become the actual designers of their ideal product, service, system, facility, or other object. Users not only specify the ideal characteristics they want, but they also design, to the extent they are able, what it will look like (its structure) and how they will use it (the process). Often, they also own the implementation. The users' initial design choices reveal user-valued priorities and opportunities. Solution providers and users then work closely to develop a prototype, modify it iteratively based on feedback from a wider group, and then execute the users' design. Using this approach, providers capture more than "the voice of the customer." They capture "the design of the customer."

Note that we said design by users is effective in supportive environments. If management is against empowering employees/users and truly employee/user-driven design, then it can be much more difficult to create the desired engagement. Designing by users in a non-supportive environment could actually make things worse by creating false hope that leads to cynicism and disengagement.

Whether your users are internal employees, external customers, or community constituents, you can easily build engagement after your solution is launched by giving users an easy way to submit ideas for improvements. Microsoft pioneered this approach in software development in the 1980s. The software giant used multiple channels to generate new product ideas from users. Before the World Wide Web existed, Microsoft set up a toll-free "wish" line for users to phone in their wishes for new software features. It also created a "wish fax" template that people could fill in, print out, and fax in. These wishes were captured in central databases. Product teams then reviewed the gold mine of ideas and implemented novel functionality in subsequent releases. In a sense, Microsoft was using "crowdsourcing" before crowdsourcing was even a term.

Microsoft is not alone in recognizing user ideas and insights as a potent source for improving products and services. Cross-industry studies have shown that users are the best single source of new ideas for products and services. For example, MIT Professor Eric von Hippel traced the origins of commercial innovations in semiconductors and found that users were the source of 63% of the major functional improvements.[4]

User-focused teams should create easy ways for users to submit their ideas and wishes that come from daily usage. USAA, the insurance and financial services company that serves military personnel and their families is another pioneer in collecting user wishes. (USAA is consistently ranked among the most customer friendly companies.) Courteous phone agents are trained to listen for unmet customer needs, which they enter into a database that is reviewed by product managers. The CEO from 1993 to 2000, Bob Herres, personally reviewed analyses of short surveys on a weekly basis, and personally responded to many letters received from customers. As a retired four-star general, he understood the importance of communicating and listening, and created a culture to support those.

USAA's practice of listening to customers has reduced the need for expensive market research studies because the employees remain closest to the users. Based on its listening processes, USAA developed numerous successful new products, generating substantial new business and increased

---

[4] von Hippel et al., *Harvard Business Review*, Sep-Oct 1999.

membership over the years. For example, by listening to customers' requests for convenient depositing, it introduced the ability to deposit checks from anywhere, first by using a scanner, and later in a mobile app.

We have been able to successfully apply Microsoft's and USAA's wish submission approaches in several settings. We applied the approach of collecting daily usage ideas to software enhancement within GlaxoSmithKline. On the systems we created, we added a wish submission form that allows users to submit enhancement ideas. On the form is a "thank you" and a statement of the importance of user wishes to improving the product. The figure below shows an example of this form.

The system features a database that automatically captures the submitted wishes, enabling easy review by the teams. Depending on the product, the team reviews could occur daily, weekly, or monthly. Typically, one person on the team is responsible for managing a process of reviewing the ideas, looking for and highlighting opportunities, and working with other team members to identify priorities.

Amazon.com draws heavily on user ideas as part of its goal to be the most customer-centric company in the world. It was recently ranked #1 in a Harris poll on companies most respected by customers. We have personally had some interaction with Amazon, as customers. Here is the response to a suggestion we submitted regarding its Amazon Prime online video service.

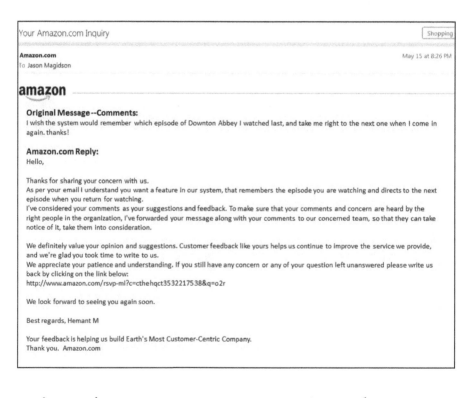

Amazon's response engages us as customers because we know the company is listening to us and welcoming our ideas. Moreover, Amazon also improves its services, further driving engagement. Even if the company is already working on this idea or already has it in place, its customer response advances engagement.

Some companies including Starbucks and Salesforce.com are using robust online platforms to engage customers. In 2008 Starbucks implemented an online idea crowdsourcing interface named My Starbucks Idea. The system not only allows customers to submit ideas, but also lets them see others' ideas, vote on ideas, comment on ideas, and see the status of ideas, including ones that have been implemented. Starbucks describes the process succinctly as "Share. Vote. Discuss. See."

MyStarbucksIdea.com

Share. Vote. Discuss. See.

 **STARBUCKS IDEA**

You know better than anyone else what you want from Starbucks. So tell us. What's your Starbucks Idea? Revolutionary or simple – we want to hear it. Share your ideas, tell us what you think of other people's ideas and join the discussion. We're here, and we're ready to make ideas happen. Let's get started.

Submit Your Idea

Below is an example of an idea that was submitted and then commented on by another customer. Customers can give an idea a thumbs up or a thumbs down.

....

| Vote | **App enhancement - 1/2 caf coffee option** | Share 📘 📷 ➕ |

👍

👎

30
points

Posted on 11/14/2016 12:29 PM
by nc4jc

Please include in your mobile ordering app the option to request 1/2 decaf coffee, in addition to dark roast, etc. I am unable to drink full caffinated coffee, so will always order 1/2 decaf in the morning. I like using the mobile order feature yet am currently unable to use it for my coffee drinks. Please add this feature to your app.

💬 Comments [1]

💬 Hide Comments [1]

pztpa

1/27/2017 4:54 AM

I am with you. Now that most Starbucks have stopped brewing decaf, a full decaf drip coffee is done one at a time using a pourover and it's very slow (rarely ready when I arrive at the store) and is always lukewarm by the time it's done.

Here is an example of Starbucks' implementation of a frequently requested idea:

Almondmilk is here!
August 08, 2016
by **blogs_nickd**

I am thrilled to announce that almondmilk, one of the top My Starbucks Idea requests of all time , will arrive in our US stores this September. Starting September 6, Starbucks Almondmilk will be available in more than 4,600 company-operated and licensed stores in the Pacific Northwest, Northern California, New York, Northeast and Mid-Atlantic regions, kicking off a nationwide rollout that will be complete by the end of September. Our almondmilk was developed by the Starbucks R&D team to pair perfectly with our hot, iced and Frappuccino® blended beverages. It is creamy and delicious with a pleasant nutty flavor and only 3 grams of sugar per 8 ounce serving. One of my favorite ways to enjoy … more »

💬 25 comments   🏷 Coming Soon, Coffee & Espresso Drinks

This powerful example demonstrates that users have a voice and, when that voice is used collectively, the company will respond, driving both customer engagement and sales.

Summarizing unhealthy practice -- Avoiding disengagement:

We added this short "unhealthy practice" section to some chapters in order to compare unhealthy with healthy practices. Perhaps it will help you recognize some of the unhealthy practices currently occurring in your own organization.

There are many ways your employees or customers can become disengaged: Sometimes a small group in your company makes all of the key decisions, which intentionally, or more often unintentionally, excludes others in the organization whose responsibilities to manage, design or implement will be impacted by the decisions. Executives in private spaces on a separate floor or building can become disconnected from the realities of the frontline business. When employees believe a project is doomed from the start, they disengage. Poor quality work and disillusionment can result when business line staff is not involved in the setting of aggressive timelines, inadequate funding, and overly ambitious scope. Another source of disengagement is when managers believe they know best and that involving those others would only slow progress.

What you could do to promote engagement:

The key message from this chapter is to go as far as you can when it comes to engaging your employees or other internal or external users such as customers or community constituents.

Organize user sessions to involve as many people as is feasible and keep the employees or users involved throughout the design of the solution. Ask the users—frequently—how the product or service ought to be. Even say, "If you could have whatever you wanted, what would it be?" Personal visits, telephone calls, meetings, emails, Web site idea/feedback buttons, and social media can all be used to collect user input. Let the users drive the detailed design of what they would like in a product, service, system, or facility. For example, you could allow users to draw out screens or diagrams, develop flows, develop prototypes, and iteratively enhance them. Allowing users to lead the design does not mean that experts don't have a role. They do, but they should first be listeners and then later collaborators who refine new ideas or solutions once the non-experts have taken things as far as they can.

Creating ways to capture ongoing employee/user wishes, such as using wish buttons on systems and/or web or intranet sites, can also be powerful in promoting engagement and, in our experience, excitement about a system, a process, product, or service. If you do create a way for people to submit wishes, make sure that you have people in place to review and push for implementation of feasible ideas. If you use an online ideas platform, list the ideas that have been implemented so people see that suggestions are taken seriously.

2. Work Backwards from Where You Want to Be

"Results are gained by exploiting opportunities, not by solving problems."

Peter Drucker

As we discussed, involving your users in designing solutions is a powerful way to foster engagement. What is even more powerful is combining user-designed solutions with a transformation process developed at Bell Laboratories in 1951. The research and development arm of the Bell Telephone system in the 20th century, Bell Laboratories is arguably the most impactful R&D organization in history. Its labs invented the transistor (semiconductors), satellites, digital audio signals (using the 1's and 0's that helped revolutionize computing), the UNIX operating system, the C programming language, radio astronomy, and lasers. Bell Labs' Walter Shewhart founded the quality movement in the 1920's by using statistics to control telephone equipment manufacturing processes. (W. Edwards Deming, the famous statistician and quality educator, did a summer internship at Bell Labs.) Bell Labs encouraged interaction and collaboration among employees with a wide range of knowledge, experience, and backgrounds. For example, one would have seen metallurgists, theoretical physicists, mathematicians, and telephone pole climbers working together on a project.

Bell Labs came up with a breakthrough approach to design and problem solving that we have found to be coincidentally quite powerful in promoting employee and user engagement. In a 1951 meeting, Bell Laboratories President Mervin Kelly told his lab section heads that Bell Labs was not innovative enough. Kelly believed the labs were too focused on removing deficiencies in the existing system, which was holding back innovation. He told them that they would achieve more breakthroughs by pretending that the phone system had been destroyed last night. Their mandate was to design the ideal phone system, the system they would want if they could have whatever they wanted. Kelly created working teams tasked with designing various aspects of the ideal phone system. One team, the telephone handset team, worked on ideas that eventually became known as speakerphones, conference calling, caller ID, answering machines, video conferencing, document sharing, call forwarding, and the push buttons that replaced the rotary dial. These obviously made a huge impact on the phone system as well as the bottom line of Bell Telephone.

Dr. Russell Ackoff, a management educator who participated in the 1951 meeting, quickly grasped the power of Kelly's "start-from-scratch" approach and turned it into a transformative methodology named "idealized design." Over the ensuing decades, the approach produced breakthrough ideas and results in many organizations including IKEA, DuPont, GlaxoSmithKline, Anheuser-Busch, The White House Communications Agency, Merck, and Boeing.

The key mechanism of idealized design is that participants pretend that the process, system, product, or service they are designing was destroyed, and they are starting over, designing their ideal replacement, one that would encompass what they *ideally want today* if they could have whatever they want.   This approach frees people to "think outside the box," unleashing creativity and generating momentum, buy-in, and consensus that support the execution of innovations and breakthroughs.   In essence, participants start at the end – where they want to be – and then work backwards from there. This approach removes perceived obstacles and generates consensus and commitment on "how to get there."

Idealized design can provide the following benefits:

- *It fosters competitive advantage* by creating a strong basis for the company and its business partners to leapfrog the competition.

- *It builds consensus* because it encourages people to focus on what's ultimately desired, their ideal rather than "how to get there."

- *It facilitates implementation* because the people who participate in designing something feel ownership for the design.

- *It creates a larger concept of what is feasible.*

- *It identifies opportunities to improve the bottom line.*

- *It is fun!* People use their imaginations and become designers. The positive atmosphere that results is energizing and encouraging.

Idealized design has produced results in many applications since it revolutionized the telephone system starting in 1951. For example, we led a project for IKEA where we combined idealized design and design by the users. IKEA's CEO for North America, Goran Carstedt, wanted to improve the shopping experience and improve same-store sales. At the time, customers expressed some frustration about the time and confusion of navigating through the store to get to what they wanted to buy.

Intrigued by idealized design, Carstedt asked us (including colleague Susan Ciccantelli) to engage 90 customers in designing their ideal IKEA shopping experience. So, instead of having the customers start from the existing store design and try to put up better signage or make more staff available to tell them how to get to the item they are looking for, idealized design got them to work backwards by having them first design what they ideally wanted.

The customers wanted to be able to quickly find items and then easily get to the checkout. They conceived an octagonal building with a central hub, allowing easy access via ramps to all of the departments located along the sides of the octagon. They illustrated their concept as far as they could, then professional architects modified the design. The architects kept the octagonal layout, but replaced the ramps with escalators that would let customers keep their carts next to them on a parallel track (see pictures below). A store built following this model in the Chicago suburb of Schaumburg, Illinois, is successful both financially and in terms of customer satisfaction. We learned that the store's sales are three times that of a conventionally-designed IKEA building in another market. Surveys put customer engagement very high. Fully 93% of customers say they would "definitely or probably shop at IKEA again." 85% of customers rated the shopping experience "excellent or very good," and 15% rated it "good." None rated it "fair or poor." Despite the store design's success, only one was built. Carstedt, who had been the model's champion, left the company for another opportunity, but did say that this store design was one of the accomplishments of which he was most proud.

Summarizing unhealthy practice -- Avoiding disengagement:

Idealized design creates more engagement when as many people as possible are involved. Avoid including just a small group of people in the process. Additionally, idealized design is not as effective when the users or people doing the actual work are not included. Avoid having others represent their voice. Since idealized design is empowering, it is often not embraced by autocratic managers. They will feel threatened by the approach and may try to undermine the efforts.

What you could do to promote engagement:

Involve as many employees or users in designing solution(s) as feasible. Instruct them to start from scratch and focus on their ideal. They should think big! Once they have come up with the overriding concepts and design, remember the motto, "Think big then start small." Identify one or more projects that can be implemented within days or weeks or several months. This will enable people, including management, to see progress and thus reinforce their engagement.

Unfortunately, we have seen too many failed projects that have dragged on for more than a year or two with no tangible results, leading to reduced engagement. If you undertake a longer-term project, such as a complex design or redesign that will take more than a few months, remember to include a number of quick-win projects that are aligned with it. People will be encouraged to stay involved if they see progress in a short timeframe.

Also, keep your employees or users involved in the design of solutions after the idealized design has been developed. In the next chapter, we discuss a way to involve people on teams that implement the ideas and designs.

For those interested in detailed how-to information on idealized design, see *Idealized Design: Dissolving Tomorrow's Crisis Today* by Russell Ackoff, Jason Magidson, and Herb Addison. See also "Shift Your Customers into Wish Mode," a chapter on idealized design in the book *PDMA Toolbook 2 for New Product Development.*

3. Enlist a Volunteer Army

John Kotter, a professor emeritus of Harvard Business School and a recognized expert in change management, recommends using a "volunteer army" as a change management lever. The idea is to establish and engage an informal network of people from multiple levels and departments who want to drive change. We have found this approach to be a powerful way to promote engagement. Kotter's volunteer army concept is part of an eight-step change management methodology he developed after researching failed and successful change efforts. The eight steps, as described recently by Kotter[5], are:

1. *Create a sense of urgency. Help others see the need for change through a bold, aspirational opportunity statement that communicates the importance of acting immediately.*
2. *Build a guiding coalition. A volunteer army needs a coalition of effective people – born of its own ranks – to guide it, coordinate it, and communicate its activities.*
3. *Form a strategic vision and initiatives. Clarify how the future will be different from the past and how you*

---

[5] http://www.kotterinternational.com/8-steps-process-for-leading-change/

....

can make that future a reality through initiatives linked directly to the vision.

4. ***Enlist a volunteer army.*** *Large-scale change can only occur when massive numbers of people rally around a common opportunity. They must be bought-in and urgent to drive change – moving in the same direction.*

5. ***Enable action by removing barriers.*** *Removing barriers such as inefficient processes and hierarchies provides the freedom necessary to work across silos and generate real impact.*

6. ***Generate short-term wins.*** *Wins are the molecules of results. They must be recognized, collected and communicated – early and often – to track progress and energize volunteers to persist.*

7. ***Sustain acceleration.*** *Press harder after the first successes. Your increasing credibility can improve systems, structures and policies. Be relentless in initiating change after change until the vision is a reality.*

8. ***Institute change.*** *Articulate the connections between the new behaviors and organizational success, making sure they continue until they become strong enough to replace old habits.*

Each of Kotter's eight steps is important to achieve change and transformation. We recommend that you try Kotter's eight steps. We could talk at length about each of those, but here we focus on step four, enlisting a volunteer army, due to its direct impact on engagement. Allowing people to volunteer for change and improvement efforts is a powerful lever for promoting engagement. Among other things, volunteering provides a sense of challenge and accomplishment that are keys to engagement.

In our improvement initiatives, we have combined the idealized design and volunteer army approaches, multiplying the impact on business results and engagement. In one initiative, we engaged all 70 employees in a transaction processing department in half-day idealized design sessions. We then reviewed the outputs documents from these sessions and identified 14 process improvement working teams. We placed 14 sheets of flipchart paper on the walls, and on each sheet we wrote the team's name, some examples of improvements the teams might work on, and spaces to sign up to volunteer to be on a team. We instructed people to sign up for their top three choices (putting a 1, 2, or 3 next to those choices), and told them we would try to get them onto their first- or second-choice team.

After working for several months, the teams achieved a 12% cost reduction in transaction processing ($660K savings) in the first year alone. The increase in efficiency supported sales growth without needing to hire additional staff. The impact on the employees was even more profound. Those who volunteered were exhilarated by their involvement, formed a robust, collaborative and proactive culture, and became enthusiastically engaged in their work. The human impact was uplifting. One early-career participant wrote:

> *I want to sincerely thank you for all that you have taught me over the past months. You have truly inspired me to bring creative thinking and effective collaboration to my everyday work and for that I will always be grateful. I know firsthand that you have impacted many of us here and your work will*

....

surely live on no matter where each of us may end up ...

Another illustrative example of combining idealized design and a volunteer army comes from a health insurance company. The company's credentialing department makes sure medical providers in its network have a valid medical license, are not excluded from doing business with the government, have liability insurance and relevant board certifications, and so on. The department engaged a facilitator from the company's transformation team to lead and coach a process improvement project, with a goal of implementing several "quick-wins." They started with idealized design sessions that included all 55 members of the department. The staff identified the ideal way they wanted the credentialing process to work and then worked backwards from that design and identified quick-win projects that could be implemented within about three months. The credentialing associates were then given the opportunity to volunteer to participate on one of eight sub-teams set up to implement the quick win projects. The volunteering aspect was important because it helped ensure people were self-motivated to participate in the sub-team they chose.

The sub-teams were chaired by the transformation facilitator and each met weekly. A steering team, consisting of sub-team leads, also met weekly and was chaired by the facilitator. The overall project produced a number of quick wins including a new training guide, a more efficient way to route phone calls, a 15-month vision that called for the hiring of a full-time trainer (which happened), standardization of the credentialing system (also accomplished), and earlier engagement of the credentialing department in the new market expansion process. (This happened too.)

Establishing a volunteer army brings several advantages:

- Volunteers bring much more energy and engagement when they can choose what they are working on.
- Teams of volunteers, rather than "volun-tolds," tend to have fewer negative, status quo maintainers who would drag down the rest of the team.
- Volunteers are able to act on motivations that may have been hampered by their current job responsibilities. For instance, employees may volunteer because they want to advance their careers or to have more impact. They may want to use a skill that has been previously unrecognized by the organization or they may want to get more recognition for their contributions.

Summarizing unhealthy practice -- Avoiding disengagement:

If you are a leader looking for a solution to a complex problem or opportunity, do not be afraid of losing control or the breakdown of hierarchy. Empowering people to come up with solutions does not diminish your power to get things done; it increases it.

What you could do to promote engagement:

Understanding how to manage change is essential to getting employee or customer engagement. About change in general, it has been said that 20% of people will be supporters, 60% will be fence sitters, and 20% will be against it. Don't worry about including the people who are against change in the volunteer army. At the start, it may actually be better to let them choose to stay on the sidelines. We have found that one can start working with supporters to make a difference, and that difference will start to win over some of the others. We were once involved in a system implementation project where we couldn't get some stakeholder groups to participate sincerely. After four months working with supporters, we launched a first iteration system, which was well liked and built our credibility. Three months later we were on the verge of implementing second generation functionality. That was when the previously disinterested groups came to us and asked to get involved. They had heard from others that even more change was coming and it was very real. They may have realized the train was leaving the station.

We recommend the following high-level steps when enlisting a volunteer army to make improvements:

1. Run one or more idealized design sessions first.
2. Identify top themes from the idealized design sessions (e.g., big opportunity areas).
3. Form teams around the top themes.
4. Use paper or electronic signup sheets for people to volunteer to be on a team. Choose a lead and co-lead for each team.
5. Create a steering team to coordinate the working teams. The steering team should include the lead and co-lead from each working team as well as a facilitator, and possibly also some members of management.
6. The working teams should identify short-term, moderate-term, and long-term actions, projects, and/or programs to move the organization to where it wants to be (from where it is today).

We have used this approach many times, and we are continually amazed by how energized and engaged people become when they are asked to participate and when leadership is supportive.

4. Involve Employees in Idea Generation and Problem Solving

"When the world is at its best, when we are at our best, when life is at its fullest, one and one equals three."

Bruce Springsteen

Ed Catmull is the cofounder and president of Pixar, the movie studio that created Toy Story, Monsters Inc., Up, A Bug's Life, and Finding Nemo. In his book, *Creativity, Inc.*,[6] he discusses how they shut down Pixar for a day and engaged virtually the entire workforce at Pixar in idea generation and problem solving. Pixar named this process "Notes Day," a reference to the candid feedback "notes" they write about their movies currently in production.

Pixar's impetus for creating Notes Day was threefold: movie production costs were increasing; external forces were putting pressure on their business; and many employees were hesitant to speak up when they had ideas. At the time,

---

[6] *Creativity, Inc.: Overcoming the Unseen Forces That Stand in the Way of True Inspiration*. Ed Catmull and Amy Wallace. Random House. 2014.

it was taking about 22,000 person weeks to make Pixar's movies. The executive leadership wanted to reduce this by about 10%. Management believed that no simple solution or single big idea would solve the three problems. When one vice president suggested that they reach out to the entire workforce for ideas, the rest of the management team got excited. They knew that good ideas could come from anyone, anywhere, and giving people time to generate ideas would energize them and generate options. Reaching out to include everyone was brilliant. Besides helping to generate ideas that would solve the cost and financial problems, it also would change the culture by encouraging everyone to speak up, become excited about the impact they could make, and become highly engaged.

Here's how Pixar's first Notes Day in 2013 worked. Ed Catmull identified a leader and team that would manage the Notes Day process. The leader formed a hands-on working team that quickly expanded as dozens of volunteers took on specific tasks. The team initially proposed shutting Pixar down for a week while they came up with ideas and solutions. However, when they realized that a week would be too disruptive to ongoing projects, they moved to shut the company down for one day. They invited everyone in the company to participate.

Leadership scheduled several town hall meetings to discuss the idea with employees, informing them that this would be a day in which the employees tell management how to make Pixar better. Their message was: "We have a problem and we believe the only people who know what to do about it are you." They said that no other work would be done that day and that all must attend. They clarified that the sessions would not be about reducing staff or working faster or harder. The sessions would be about making the company better. Management made clear that the people doing the work had the answers.

Planning for Notes Day began months in advance. One of the first actions of the Notes Day Working Group was to set up an electronic idea box to which employees could email discussion topics for Notes Day. Employees submitted more than 1,000 ideas for improvements, innovations, enhancing workflows, and even suggestions on how to run Notes Day. The Notes Day Working Group distilled this into 120 discussion topics grouped into several categories. To get an idea of how many people would participate in each topic discussion, the Working Group surveyed employees.

To ensure Notes Day would be productive, the Working Group decided that employees would be free to attend whichever sessions they liked, and they recruited session facilitators from within the employee ranks. These facilitators were trained to ensure all session attendees were heard. Facilitators were given "exit forms" for each session that would foster next steps to take ideas forward rather than simply result in interesting discussions that may not go anywhere. Exit forms, which were tweaked for specific sessions, contained sections where participants were able to enter information including ideas for actions, proposals, benefits to the company, next steps, who should pitch proposals, and what audience they should pitch to.

When Notes Day finally arrived on March 11, 2013, nearly all employees participated. Most sessions were cross-functional because people were free to sign up for what interested them. The session "Developing and Appreciating a Great Workplace" included a participant from Finance, Systems, Legal, an animator, and a chef. To prompt the team's thinking, its exit form asked: "It's 2017. Nobody at the studio behaves as if they are entitled. How did we accomplish that?"

This team discussed helping staff learn more about what other employees do so they could understand the big picture and not criticize others. Their proposals for getting to know each other better across the company included a job-swapping program, a lunch lottery, and cross-departmental mixers. Thinking back to our chapter on culture, it occurs to us that these are good ways to help shift a culture from "I'm great and you're not" to "we're great together."

Throughout Notes Day and at the barbecue and beer party that followed it, Ed Catmull and his leadership team noticed that employees were energized and engaged, evidenced by their excitement and lingering conversations. In the days that followed, management received feedback from many employees, calling the process "cathartic" and asking that Notes Day be repeated the next year. "Notes Day is proof that Pixar cares about people as much as about finances," said one employee note. Another employee concluded, "I think we all walked away with a sense of ownership over this amazing place, and its future. A 'we're all in this together' feel."

Shortly after the big event, the Notes Day leadership team reviewed the exit forms that had been completed in each session. As you'll recall, each of these forms had a place where the session group could write "who should pitch this proposal" for ideas they liked. The idea was to keep the momentum for the best ideas. Ownership was baked into the situation from the start. The "idea advocates," as they called these employees, were gathered together over the following few weeks and the Notes Day leadership team helped them hone their pitches. The advocates then pitched them to the company's executive leadership team, which began implementing the ones that would result in the greatest benefits.

What you could do to promote engagement:

Catmull says three key factors led to Notes Day's success in engaging employees: 1.) The discussion topics came from the employees and they had a focus on a specific challenge the organization faced. 2.) Employees understood that Notes Day was championed by top management so they took it seriously. The fact that management was investing a full day of salary to focus on these challenges and stopping all other work was important but not even close to most important. Management was showing employees that they were supportive of them working and sharing ideas freely across functions, and that they were fully prepared to act on many ideas. 3.) Notes Day was managed by internal employees, not an outside management consultant. Employees took ownership of the process and the results.

Here are the high-level steps one can use for establishing a Notes Day:

1. Make sure Notes Day is championed from the very top of the organization.
2. Select a highly respected executive to lead the overall effort.
3. Form a Notes Day working team staffed by volunteers who are willing to take on specific tasks. (Notes Day should be managed by employees, not external consultants.)
4. Identify a specific challenge the organization faces, around which Notes Day can focus.
5. To communicate the Notes Day idea to employees, schedule town hall meetings where you tell employees

that this will be a day where they tell management how to make the company better. Clarify that the day is not about reducing staff or working faster or harder. It's about making the company better.

6. With the specific challenge in mind, collect ideas for Notes Day discussion topics from employees well in advance of Notes Day. Distill these into a workable number of sessions. To help with logistics of the day, send a survey to employees about how many people are interested in each topic discussion.

7. Allow employees to attend whatever sessions they like.

8. Identify and train facilitators for each Notes Day session.

9. Provide an "exit form" for each session where participants can write ideas for actions to take, proposals, benefits, next steps, who should pitch proposals, and audience they should pitch to.

10. Shortly after the big event, the Notes Day leadership team should review the "exit forms" that have been filled out in each session.

11. Gather "idea advocates" (i.e., those who are identified in the "exit forms" as people who will pitch the proposals) over the following few weeks and help them hone their pitches.

12. The advocates then make their pitches to the company's executive leadership team

13. Begin the process of implementing the ideas that are chosen

Part II

Customer Centricity

5. Get "Tuned In" to External Customer Needs

Being "tuned in" complements the other approaches involving users in design, identifying where you ideally want to be, using crowdsourcing, and using a volunteer army. This tuned-in approach, which creates both customer and employee engagement, is presented in the book, *Tuned In*, by Craig Stull, Phil Meyers, and David Meerman Scott. They advocate changing the prevailing culture of organizations from internally focused decision making to becoming an organization that focuses intensely on identifying and solving important problems that current and potential customers are willing to pay to for. They point out that many companies rely on "conference room decision making" wherein a small group of people make key decisions about products, services, or systems that are likely off-target from what customers really need.

Stull and his coauthors advocate for getting out in the marketplace and observing customers in their settings. One of the examples in the book is about Boeing. Blake Emery, the director of Differentiation Strategy at Boeing met with flight attendants, pilots, and frequent fliers. He not only observed them in the plane, but involved them in designing their ideal airline cabin experience. They suggested, among other things, larger windows, colored ceiling lighting to simulate the open space of the daytime or nighttime sky, better cabin pressurization and humidity, and easier ways to enter and exit the plane. Many of their ideas are being used in new-generation Boeing planes. Not only does Boeing benefit by offering a better travel experience for customers and flight personnel, but the employees who are involved have increased pride in the company's products, which enhances their engagement.

We were able to apply the concept of intense customer focus with procurement leaders at the Fort Belvoir U.S. Army base, located just outside of Washington, D.C. We were aiding a company that provides online bidding software and services that help the Army's procurement department increase competition and quality from suppliers. The commanding officer and her team gave us a gold mine of ideas for improving process efficiency and effectiveness. For example, the team said its contracting, request for proposal, and other systems weren't talking with the company's software and that they had to manually re-enter information in order to use the software. This presented a big opportunity to make things work better for the government. This opportunity was revealed because we got out of our conference rooms, went to "where the customer lives," and listened and watched. As a result, the customer became more engaged and we did too. It was exciting to know we could make a difference and recognize the potential market opportunities.

In another engagement we applied the concept of intense customer focus by meeting with physicians, nurses, and staff in primary care offices called upon by the GlaxoSmithKline sales team. We learned that the doctors, nurses, and non-clinical office staff had several pain points: 1.) The process of helping patients get prescriptions filled was an administrative burden on both the office and the patient; 2.) Doctors and nurses believed that patients needed more education on conditions such as diabetes, high blood pressure, and heart disease; 3.) Doctors were open to the sales force providing them studies from trusted medical journals; and 4.) Office staff wanted help with how to use their office systems in conjunction with those of various healthcare insurers and providers.

With this knowledge about the physician groups, we then went back into GlaxoSmithKline and worked with the vice president of sales training and her team to transform the sales training department. We engaged her customers — the sales representatives — in designing the ideal sales training program. We advised that she have her sales training team sit in on those sessions as silent observers. Here is a sampling of what they heard:

- Use in-person sales force training time for role playing and conversational selling, rather than in-person lectures. Move the lecture content to online modules that sales reps can complete ahead of time.
- Assign a veteran sales mentor to each new rep for six months to help them get started and become successful.
- Provide new reps with education on the psychology of success.

The VP and her team would then be able to take the outputs and hold similar sessions where they, themselves, design their ideal sales training program. This project was a win-win because her team embraced the input of the physician offices and the design of the sales force, incorporating most of it into their program. In this fashion, we generated both a high customer focus and a high level of team engagement.

In addition to connecting with user needs in person, there are many ways companies can identify unmet needs through social and other electronic media. For example, product feedback on online sites such as Amazon.com can provide many ideas for product improvement. Social media comments are also a robust source. Additionally, as we mention elsewhere in the book, companies such as Starbucks are using idea crowdsourcing software for identifying opportunities to satisfy unmet customer needs and desires.

Summarizing unhealthy practice -- Avoiding disengagement:

Avoid making key decisions about what to do for customers or users based on limited or no interaction with them. No customer input often leads to failure, lower morale, and reduced engagement.

What you could do to promote engagement:

There are several practices that will help you get tuned in:

- Adopt a philosophy of identifying the most important needs and problems among your customers and those you would like to be your customers.
- Go out into the world with some colleagues and observe your customers using your product or service. Watch and listen for issues and unmet needs. Ask what could be improved.

- Provide your customers with a way to submit wishes for solutions. Provide opportunities for some customers to design what they would like.
- Share insights gained with others in your organization.
- Incorporate into your organization's core values a statement about how you will have a customer problem seeking and solving culture.
- Last but not least, you can enhance your customer-problem-solving focus by using a customer idea crowdsourcing solution.

6. Focus on Extraordinary Internal Customer Service

"If you're not serving the customer, your job is to be serving someone who is."

Jan Carlzon

"There's a remarkably close and consistent link between how internal customers are treated and how external customers perceive the quality of your organization's services. A commitment to serve internal customers invariably shows itself to external customers. It's almost impossible to provide good external service if your organization is not providing good internal service."

Benjamin Schneider, University of Maryland

This short chapter can serve as an adjunct to the chapters on creating visions and actively creating a desirable culture. As we've discussed, a work environment in which it is difficult to accomplish much contributes to low employee engagement. We have found that one of the root causes is departmental leaders who do not see themselves as dedicated "collaborator servants" to other departments' efforts to make progress. They see their departments more as their power bases, and often resist and/or are "offended" by other departments' complaints about inadequate service.

Anyone in a department, including its leaders, could make an incredible contribution to employee engagement and serve external customers. The key is to shift their team's attitude and culture to focus on providing extraordinary "internal customer service" to other departments that serve external customers. The resulting accomplishments could quickly start to turn around morale and engagement.

Summarizing unhealthy practice -- Avoiding disengagement:

Avoid viewing your department or team as more important than others. Avoid seeking power for power's sake over other departments.

What you could do to promote engagement:

In addition to the levers discussed in other chapters (e.g., create core values and a vision for your function or organization), you could actively seek ideas that would help your internal customers, and then start working on ideas that would produce quick wins. Create a culture and an expectation that internal groups that do not directly serve an external customer will serve those that are. Even if other departments are not focused on serving their internal customers, you can begin to change this dynamic by leading through example.

7. De-Emphasize Internally Focused Metrics and Quotas

"So much of what we call management consists of making it difficult for people to work."

Peter Drucker

In many organizations, people are held back from intensely focusing on the needs of external customers and from giving great service to other internal departments. One reason is that their departments become too focused on internal metrics and quotas. Examples include: You must complete a minimum of 25 customer files per week or you are rated as nonperforming; your average length of customer phone call must not exceed five minutes; you must close out an IT service ticket within three days; you must complete 300 customer-record update requests per week.

Many IT help desks demonstrate the negative effects of quotas. They are frequently more focused on closing the ticket vs. solving the customer's problem. Even when they need to forward or elevate a customer issue to another group, they want to close the ticket.

In theory quotas and metrics help performance. In practice, however, we've seen performance drop through disengagement, through excessive administrative burden, as well as through destructive behaviors. For example, the people who are required to complete 25 customer files per week mark things complete even though they didn't have time to do everything correctly; employees responsible for updating 300 customer records make the requested update, but don't have time to fix incorrect information such as an outdated customer address that they notice while they are in the record. This neglect leads to delays and rework whenever mail is sent to this inaccurate address.

Many companies measure length of time on a call to resolve a customer's issue. Consequently, employees who are worried about penalties for staying on calls too long will be tempted to transfer, bouncing the customer around. In contrast, Zappos does not measure length of calls. They encourage and empower their employees to do what they need to do to ensure the customer is delighted. They know that the external metric of customer delight is much more important.

Some managers implement quotas so they can manage their "poor performers." We understand the desire to get people's performance up or to push out those who are not performing. However, quotas can also have unanticipated consequences of pulling the team's focus away from customers and cross-functional collaboration. There are alternatives to quotas and intense focus on internal metrics. Some companies avoid creating quotas and internally focused metrics by designing ways for employees to flexibly find roles they love and in which they excel. The employees are able to evaluate each other, which helps reveal poor performance. We elaborate on this in the chapter, "Allow Employee Autonomy."

We recommend de-emphasizing or eliminating many, if not most of your internally focused metrics and quotas, which tend to alienate employees from their work.

It is not only in businesses where internally focused metrics create problems. Metrics adversely affect student engagement in the educational system. In many countries, extensive testing and measurement has driven much of the joy out of learning. In the name of accountability, many in power have pushed for tougher standards and more rigorous testing. However, humans are not robots. Each student is unique, as each employee is unique. Students will be much more engaged when they can pursue their own interests and passions for learning. There are some educational thinkers (e.g., Alfie Kohn and Dan Greenberg) and schools (e.g., schools modeled after the Sudbury Valley School) that advocate against testing and measurement.

What you could do to promote engagement:

Instead of overdoing measurement, believe in your people. We encourage our teams to listen to their customers and then do what will delight them. If you want to use metrics, use global measures that tie to intrinsic motivation such as Net Promoter Score, a type of customer satisfaction tool. It compares what percentage of customers are saying good things about the organization (i.e., promoting it) with the percentage that are saying bad things about the organization. Metrics should focus on external factors such as customer satisfaction, regulatory requirements, and contractual obligations.

Part III

Culture Matters

8. Actively Create a Desirable Culture

The Merriam-Webster Dictionary defines culture as shared beliefs, shared social forms, shared features of everyday existence, and shared attitudes, values, goals, and practices. It also defines it as shared conventions or social practices.

A group is often not aware of its culture because culture develops over time. An example of culture in an organizational setting is how staff or departments interact with each other. Do they ignore each other? Compete with each other? Or collaborate with each other? Other examples of culture include whether all people have an opportunity to contribute ideas and participate in problem solving; whether people are regularly recognized for their contributions; whether work and fun go together; whether the organization is intensely user driven.

Culture is an incredibly powerful determinant of employees' engagement. A great culture does not happen by accident; it requires effort and determination. Let's look again at the example of online retailer Zappos.com, a wholly-owned subsidiary of Amazon.com led by Tony Hsieh (pronounced s-h-a-y). In his fascinating book, *Delivering Happiness,* Tony discusses his journey to the leadership of a company whose employee morale and dedication to delighting its customers is extraordinary. He explains that he learned how to shape that culture by recognizing the mistakes he made at LinkExchange, a Silicon Valley tech startup that he cofounded and then sold to Microsoft for $265 million at the age of 24. Tony's share of the sale was $32 million in cash plus another $8 million for staying with the company during a 12-month transition. However, Tony became so disenchanted with LinkExchange's culture that he left the company before the 12 months ended, walking away from the $8 million. He wrote that bitter internal conflicts led to numerous dysfunctions within the company. He blamed himself for the bad culture because he had not consciously created an explicit company culture, allowing an accidental culture to emerge. Tony concluded that to become a great company, the desired culture must be shaped through an explicit focus.

Tony decided to focus intensely on creating a great culture in his next venture. With his money from the sale of his company, he created a venture capital company that funded the fledgling Zappos.com. Tony became deeply involved with the company, eventually becoming CEO. Growing the start-up business was challenging. Tony burned through nearly his entire $32 million financing the venture and acquiring a supply of shoes to meet orders.

True to his word, Tony focused intensely on creating a great culture. One of the levers was to come up with core values that guide behavior and decisions. Here is a recent list of Zappos' core values:

Zappos 10 Core Values

At Zappos our 10 Core Values are more than just words, they're a way of life. We know that companies with a strong culture and a higher purpose perform better in the long run. As we continue to grow, we strive to ensure that our culture remains alive and well. Check out our core values and see if they speak to you.

Our 10 Core Values

1. Deliver WOW Through Service
2. Embrace and Drive Change
3. Create Fun and A Little Weirdness
4. Be Adventurous, Creative, and Open-Minded
5. Pursue Growth and Learning
6. Build Open and Honest Relationships With Communication
7. Build a Positive Team and Family Spirit
8. Do More With Less
9. Be Passionate and Determined
10. Be Humble

To see how Zappos elaborates on each of these core values, let's take a look at the company's drill-down on two of them, *Deliver WOW Through Service* and *Be Passionate and Determined*:

At Zappos, anything worth doing is worth doing with WOW.

WOW is such a short, simple word, but it really encompasses a lot of things. To WOW, you must differentiate yourself, which means doing something a little unconventional and innovative. You must do something that's above and beyond what's expected. And whatever you do must have an emotional impact on the receiver. We are not an average company, our service is not average, and we don't want our people to be average. We expect every employee to deliver WOW.

Whether internally with co-workers or externally with our customers and partners, delivering WOW results in word of mouth. Our philosophy at Zappos is to WOW with service and experience, not with anything that relates directly to monetary compensation (for example, we don't offer blanket discounts or promotions to customers).

We seek to WOW our customers, our co-workers, our vendors, our partners, and in the long run, our investors.

Passion is the fuel that drives us and our company forward.

We value passion, determination, perseverance, and the sense of urgency.

"We are inspired because we believe in what we are doing and where we are going. We don't take "no" or "that'll never work" for an answer because if we had, then Zappos would have never started in the first place.

Passion and determination are contagious. We believe in having a positive and optimistic (but realistic) attitude about everything we do because we realize that this inspires others to have the same attitude.

There is excitement in knowing that everyone you work with has a tremendous impact on a larger dream and vision, and you can see that impact day in and day out.

We find these core values to be thoroughly inspiring. We particularly like the emphasis on going above and beyond what is expected, especially making an emotional impact on the customer. This ignites the humanity, excitement, and motivation to act, makes employees feel alive, and helps them build off of each other's inspiring actions.

What do you think the chances are of getting this level of commitment from employees if you are not explicitly asking for it? Pretty low, right? In our experience, without asking for this kind of cultural behavior, you are more likely to get dysfunctional behavior. In contrast, when most of the people around you are trying to WOW fellow employees and customers, you have a very exciting environment where you are inspired to rise to the level of expectation.

Zingerman's is another extraordinary business that is very explicit about its core values and their central role in achieving a thriving business and employee engagement. Zingerman's, based in Ann Arbor, Michigan, started in 1982 as a delicatessen and grew into "a community of businesses" with roughly $50 million in annual sales. Its original vision was to create a great corned beef sandwich. Zingerman's community of businesses now includes a coffee company, a confectionary business, a bread business, restaurants, and a food mail-order business.

Zingerman's refers to its core values as its guiding principles.

Guiding Principles

So, how do we bring the Zingerman's Experience to as many people as possible? We hit our 3 Bottom Lines and we live by our Guiding Principles. The Guiding Principles talk about how we work together, how we relate to each other, to our guests, to our suppliers, to our community. These principles are at the core of everything we do; they drive our decision making, they help us with our planning, and they guide us in our daily work. We hope that during the time that you are here you will help us to build on, revise, refine and strengthen Zingerman's Guiding Principles. We successfully share the Zingerman's Experience by following our principles and living our commitment to providing and/or building:

1. Great Food!
2. Great Service!
3. A Great Place to Shop and Eat!
4. Solid Profits!
5. A Great Place to Work!
6. Strong Relationships!
7. A Place to Learn!
8. An Active Part of Our Community!

Although we would like to reproduce all eight guiding principles here, they are a bit lengthy, so we include two of them to give you a feel for how inspiring they are.

Guiding Principle 2. Great Service!

We go the x-tra mile, giving exceptional service to each guest.

We are committed to giving great service—meeting the guests' expectations and then exceeding them. Great service like this is at the core of the Zingerman's Experience. Our guests always leave with a sense of wonderment at how we have gone out of our way to make their experience at Zingerman's a rewarding one.

Our bottom line is derived from customer satisfaction.

Customer satisfaction is the fuel that stokes the Zingerman's fire. If our guests aren't happy, we're not happy. To this end, we consistently go the x-tra mile— literally and figuratively—for our guests. The customer is never an interruption in our day. We welcome feedback of all sorts. We constantly reevaluate our performance to better accommodate our customers. Our goal is to have our guests leave happy. Each of us takes full responsibility for making our guest's experience an enjoyable one before, during and after the sale.

We believe that giving great service is an honorable profession.

Quality service is a dignified and honorable pursuit. We take great pride in our ability to provide our guests and our staff with exceptional service. Service is about giving and caring for those around us.

We give great service to each other as well as to our guests.

We provide the same level of service to our peers as we do our guests. We are polite, supportive, considerate, superb listeners, and always willing to go the x-tra mile for each other.

Guiding Principle 5. A Great Place to Work!

Working at Zingerman's means taking an active part in running the business. Our work makes a difference.

We are empowered by the creativity, hard work and commitment of our staff.

It is the energy, effort and involvement of our staff that helps make Zingerman's successful. We seek to build on the creativity and intelligence of everyone here.

We are committed to each other's success.

Each of us is committed to the success of everyone else who works at Zingerman's. We support each other, listen well, facilitate and encourage each other's growth and advancement.

We compensate our staff well.

We provide income, a benefits package, profit sharing, meaningful work, and a sense of community for our staff, which balances their needs with the resources of the business.

We provide opportunity for growth and advancement.

We actively work to provide for the healthy growth of our business. In so doing, we provide opportunities for staff who wish to grow within Zingerman's.

We involve as many people as possible in the running of the business.
We bring as many people as practical into the operation of the business. In so doing, Zingerman's runs more effectively, benefiting from everyone's abilities, creativity, experience and intelligence.

Each of us is committed to being proactive in our work.
We aggressively tackle difficult issues without waiting to be asked. We know that each of us bears the responsibility for what goes on around us, and we have the opportunity and ability to effect positive change within the business.

We work to improve in every area.
We seek to improve our performance, individually and as a group, and work to our fullest potential, through self-reflection, education, cooperation and feedback from others. When something is not working, we look at ourselves to improve before we look at the work of others. We do so as individuals, as departments and businesses.

We learn from our errors and work to correct them.
When we make mistakes, we view them as opportunities for growth and change. When we make

an error we do not seek to assign blame, rather, we try
to avoid repeating the problem in the future.

We strive to create a safe workplace.
We work within the limits of our space to create a safe
workplace. We continually reevaluate and act to
improve our work space. We walk slowly and carefully
on the stairs, we never leave knives unattended in the
sink, we pay close attention at all times when using
slicers. We catch each other when we fall.

Zingerman's embraces diversity.
We go out of our way to build a diverse and well-
balanced workplace. We hire individuals regardless of
race, religion, gender or sexual preference.

We like to have fun.
And we take our fun very seriously. So don't mess with
it.

We were inspired by the work Zappos and Zingerman's are doing with core values and guiding principles to create a great culture. Their statements create a momentum that makes it hard for naysayers and critics to discourage those who want to make a difference, and leads the naysayers to move on. What a fertile environment for engagement! Think of all of the companies that do not have a culture that identifies what the company stands for. In companies not explicitly committed to creating a great culture, engaged employees who want to make a difference must fight a tougher battle to create the future they want.

Even if you are not operating across the entire company, it's easy to adopt core values. You can develop core values for a team, a department, or even for a project. For example, we adapted core values for several diverse process improvement initiatives we were leading for a health insurance plan. One was for an operations department, another was for a software development project, and the following was for the entire health plan:

> *To be a highly successful team that people want to work for and with, we feel it is important to explicitly define our core values from which we develop our culture. We live by these core values:*
>
> 1. *Be a collaborative, respectful and inclusive team — demonstrate a "we're great together" culture.*
> 2. *Create an experience for providers and members that shows our sincere concern.*
> 3. *Deeply understand whom we serve.*
> 4. *Be accountable and responsible — own it.*
> 5. *Have clearly defined roles and responsibilities.*
> 6. *Foster positive and effective communication.*
> 7. *Recognize and celebrate our successes.*
> 8. *Drive innovation and embrace change, new ideas and technologies.*
> 9. *Be dedicated to learning and providing tools, training and mentoring to our associates.*
> 10. *Last but not least, have fun!*

This core values statement actually began as part of a small project to improve service to members and medical providers. The president of the health plan became aware of the core values we were practicing in the project and said she wanted to adapt and adopt this across her entire health plan.

On another project for which we created a set of core values, we were able to put the concept into practice in other ways that enhance employee engagement. When one woman who was leading one of eight process improvement teams for the project said she would like to share an idea, a second woman bluntly said she didn't want to hear it. We calmly asked the second woman to look at Core Value Number 5 on the wall poster, and notice that it called for being collaborative, respectful, and inclusive. We also said that following the core values is the responsibility of all improvement team leads. She apologized and said, "Please, go ahead and share your idea." The core values really came in handy.

Tribal Leadership, Culture, and Engagement

There is another powerful way of looking at changing culture in order to foster employee engagement. In their book, *Tribal Leadership*, Dave Logan, John King, and Halee Fischer-Wright talk about how an organization's culture can be assessed and ultimately transformed to create not only a great place to work, where there is a high level of employee engagement, but also to potentially change the world. The authors assert that organizations consist of a number of tribes, each composed of up to 150 people. The CEOs and other leaders who can win over the tribes can be successful, hence the book's title, *Tribal Leadership*.

The authors studied 24,000 employees and identified five stages of culture, which are captured in the diagram below.

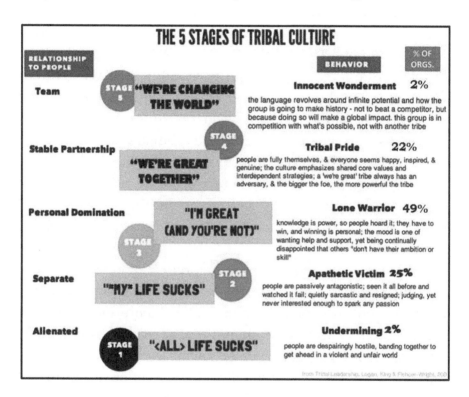

Organizations often have a blend of cultures, but the five stages, which relate to employee engagement, provide a feel for the prevalent culture in an organization.

Stage 1. This is the lowest stage. Fortunately, only about 2% of companies are at Stage 1, where people are openly hostile (sometimes violent) and undermining is prevalent. Unfortunately, people in these organizations despair, and the widespread feeling is "all life sucks."

Stage 2. About a quarter of companies are at the next stage, in which most employees have given up. They have become apathetic, passively resistant, sarcastic, and resigned. The feeling is that others may be doing well, but "my life sucks."

Stage 3. About half of companies in the United States are at Stage 3, where the predominant culture is "I'm great and you're not." This could be at the individual level or the departmental level. This is characterized by conflict, reduced cooperation, reduced trust levels, win-lose behavior, and personal domination. Those who are in power may view others as not being committed, ambitious or skillful, or carrying their weight. For those who feel they are great, they are often less than satisfied and can eventually feel burned out because they try to do too much themselves, hoard power and information, and do not build coalitions to get things done.

Stage 4. Only about one in five organizations are at Stage 4. This stage is best described as "We're great together." There is a culture of partnership and collaboration within the organization. There are shared core values and happy, engaged employees who can be themselves while making a difference together. Additionally, there is often a culture of adversarial relationships with competing organizations.

Stage 5. Only two percent of organizations are at Stage 5, which can be characterized as "Life is great" and "We're changing the world." The employees are trying to make history. Rather than competing with other organizations, they are competing with what's possible, trying to implement a remarkable vision. A famous example is NASA, with its vision and program to get man onto the moon and back safely by the end of the 1960s.

Logan and his colleagues discovered an interesting and easy way to assess an organization's or department's or project's tribal culture stage by simply listening to conversations in elevators, break rooms, cafeterias, etc. We encourage you to try this in your own organization and see what stage(s) it occupies.

A more recent example of a Stage 5 organization is the pharmaceutical company Amgen. They moved to a Stage 5 culture by viewing cancer and other diseases as its competition rather than other companies. They wanted to change the world by transforming medicine using biotechnology.

Another inspiring example from *Tribal Leadership* is Griffin Hospital in Connecticut. Griffin's chief operating officer, who went on to become CEO, got the "tribes" in the organization to buy into a vision of creating the most extraordinary patient experience. The company *engaged* all employees and numerous patients and their family members and friends in co-designing many aspects of their services. For instance, for the maternity ward they incorporated valet parking, double beds, a Jacuzzi for pain management, family rooms with kitchens, comfortable waiting areas, and 24x7 visiting hours. They also came up with core values that include quality, service, respect, and dignity.

We intentionally italicized the word engaged in the paragraph above because the act of simply engaging all of your employees in solving problems and/or coming up with a compelling vision is a powerful lever for creating overall employee engagement within the organization. In fact, Griffin Hospital achieved a ranking of fourth on *Fortune* magazine's list of the best places to work in its seventh year on the list.

Summarizing unhealthy practice -- Avoiding disengagement:

As Tony Hsieh and Ari Weinzweig have pointed out, a great culture does not happen by accident. If you want a culture that fosters employee engagement, you will need to explicitly

....

focus and put a lot of energy into creating it. Doing nothing, and hoping, will not – we repeat, *will not* create this environment.

What you could do to promote engagement:

As we discussed above, start engaging your employees in problem solving, and they will likely become more engaged in your organization.

You can take actions to win over the tribes while moving the organization to stage 4 or 5. For example, you can engage your stakeholders in creating a set of core values to drive a culture that fosters employee engagement. Don't wait for the larger organization to create core values — start where you are. If you're running a project, create core values for the project. If you're managing a department, engage your employees in creating core values for the department. If you're a member in a department, you can pitch the idea to the leader and see if he or she is open to it. If all else fails, you can create your own core values to live and work by.

To create core values, organize a group of people to brainstorm ideas. We've co-created core values with groups as small as three people and as large as 80. Once you have gotten input, you can assign one or two people to synthesize the input into a draft list of core values. For each core value, write several sentences that elaborate on and clarify it. Then circulate this document for additional feedback, keeping the document marked draft for a while so people will feel comfortable requesting improvements.

You can also listen to conversations to assess where your organization, department, team, or project places in the five stages of tribal culture, and then start to use the new core values to move it to higher stages. However, creating core values is not your only lever for creating a culture that fosters employee engagement. Although the approaches in each chapter can stand alone, the impact can be multiplied by combining them. As we discuss in another chapter, you can also create a vision that fosters alignment and inspires people to work together collaboratively, so that you can move your organization to a stage 4 or 5 culture.

Fortunately, although it helps, you don't need to have a high position in an organization to have an impact on the organization's culture. You can begin where you are — with what you manage or influence — and set an example by creating the culture you desire. We've seen this work many times. When others see the impact in a smaller area, they become open to adopting the approach in other areas.

9. Promote Diversity

"Injustice anywhere is a threat to justice everywhere. We are caught in an inescapable network of mutuality, tied in a single garment of destiny. Whatever affects one directly, affects all indirectly."

Martin Luther King Jr., Letter from the Birmingham Jail

This paragraph serves as our public service announcement. As we write this book, diversity is under attack in the United States as some so-called leaders scapegoat several minorities, playing on people's fears for political gain. We all must challenge this disgraceful and inexcusable behavior.

The movie *Hidden Figures* was released in 2016, illustrating the story of three female African American engineers who made substantial contributions to the 1960s NASA space program while enduring racial and gender discrimination. Their perseverance and key contributions to the success of the space program is an uplifting saga (pun intended).

Discrimination affects engagement. There is a growing body of research about a much more subtle, unconscious form of discrimination known as unconscious bias. We are all subject to unconscious biases that may include: discrimination based on accent, age (young or old), religious beliefs, physical or mental disabilities, race, ethnicity, language, skin color, LGBTQ status, national origin, formal education attained, gender, height, weight, body shape, physical attractiveness, level in the organizational hierarchy, introvertedness or extrovertedness, where someone grew up, or political viewpoints. There are many more.

Overcoming unconscious bias is becoming a priority for more companies. For example, Google has acknowledged a lack of diversity among its engineers, and in recent years its top executives supported the launch of a program to educate employees about unconscious bias. Their goal is to build and sustain an inclusive organizational culture.[7] Google has also made materials on unconscious bias available to the public at this link:

https://rework.withgoogle.com/subjects/unbiasing/

Google's materials help employees become aware of stereotypes and biases, explaining:

> Unconscious biases are shortcuts our brains create to deal with large amounts of information. Our brains "fill in the blanks. They "pattern map" to someone you think you should hire or put on a team or promote or put in a leadership position. Perhaps your brain unconsciously gets you to exclude someone who is not from your same background or who doesn't look or speak like you. It can be hard to see talents when you don't see that fitting what your brain expects to be true. What makes unconscious bias so hard to overcome is that people

---

[7] https://rework.withgoogle.com/subjects/unbiasing/

believe they can perceive things objectively but are statistically wrong.

We have so much to learn about discrimination and unconscious bias. Understanding unconscious bias can be a first step in helping us to enable each other to become more engaged. It is mind boggling to think about how much disengagement occurs among people excluded by unconscious bias, and the vast opportunity to promote engagement by raising awareness and changing our behaviors.

Here are a few questions that may help us think about how unconscious bias may be limiting how we promote diversity:

- How diverse is your group of friends along any of the dimensions above?
- How diverse are the people you work with and include in your "inner circle"?
- If you have hired people, how diverse have your hires been?
- Are you giving equal opportunities to diverse people?
- Which of these diverse groups have you had over to your home?

What you could do to promote engagement:
Make inclusiveness a priority wherever you are in the organization, and if possible from the very top. Learn as much as you can and educate others about unconscious bias and teach them ways to reduce it. Implementing a formal program can foster a more inclusive environment, and thereby promote engagement.

10. Build a Culture of Positive Appreciation

This chapter focuses on a powerful lever for promoting engagement: creating a culture of appreciating others. Research on motivation backs up the practice of appreciating employees. As we discuss in detail elsewhere in the book, Frederick Herzberg found that receiving recognition and being appreciated are two of the most powerful motivators.

We once again turn to Zingerman's food business, which provides an extraordinary model for appreciating employees,[8] along with a compelling rationale for doing so:

> *Being appreciative is the right thing to do from every angle. Everyone wants to feel valued; people want to know that their efforts make a difference, and that they are part of something greater than themselves. When they feel that their work is contributing positively, they are more likely to go beyond the norm. An appreciative culture sets a positive tone.*

Zingerman's does several things to promote a culture of positive appreciation:

---

[8] https://www.zingtrain.com/content/culture-positive-appreciation

1. *Teach it.* One shouldn't assume that people will naturally be appreciative of others. One needs to explicitly teach the idea of and techniques for being appreciative. The cofounder and CEO teaches the new employee orientation class, and models the desired appreciation behavior, explicitly naming the people and their actions that he appreciates. In other classes and in the course of everyday work at Zingerman's, leaders communicate to staff how they value positive appreciation and they expect the staff to do the same.

2. *Define it.* Zingerman's reinforces positive appreciation in numerous places. In its mission statement Zingerman's aspires to create a positive experience for every interaction with customers, suppliers, peers, and neighbors. Being explicit helps set the expectation. One of Zingerman's three bottom lines is Great Service, which includes "creating a positive workplace in which everyone feels valued and knows their work makes a difference." Zingerman's guiding principles state, "We give great service to each other as well as to our guests. We go the extra mile for each other. We are polite, supportive, considerate, superb listeners, working on the basis of mutual respect and care." The visioning process Zingerman's uses, which we discuss elsewhere in this book, also fosters positive and appreciative attitudes – they focus on going after what they want rather than fighting what they don't want. Zingerman's also follows a 4-to1 ratio of appreciation – four parts praise to one part constructive criticism.

A side benefit of showing appreciation is that it often makes people more accepting of constructive feedback and criticism. In fact, those who receive constructive feedback are more likely to feel that the appreciations they receive are more genuine. It's all in the spirit of continually improving.

3. *Live it.* Living it includes several recommendations:
   - Don't forget to appreciate yourself. On the path to excellence, it is helpful to take stock of and recognize yourself for what you have achieved.
   - To encourage others to appreciate fellow employees, make sure to appreciate the appreciations they are making.
   - At the end of every meeting, set aside a few minutes for appreciations – about anything or anyone; about people in the room or not; about something in the past, present, or future; and, work related or not. Doing appreciations at the end of meetings sends people away on a positive note and disciplines people to think about them regularly.
   - Include pages of appreciations in your staff newsletter.
   - Capture and share widely compliments received from customers.
   - Start performance reviews by listing the employee's achievements.
   - When appreciating, be specific rather than general.
   - Go the extra mile. Do something unexpected for the employees you appreciate, such as leaving a Post-it on their computer screen, giving them a flower, or mailing them a handwritten note.

4. *Measure it.* Zingerman's measures appreciation in various ways including through surveys. Questions include: In the past seven days have I received praise for my work? Does my supervisor or someone at work care about me as a person? Do my opinions count?

What you could do to promote engagement:

Our recommendation here is simple: In your area of influence, implement the appreciations process Zingerman's uses.

11. Connect People

Two books and one networking organization influenced our understanding of the power of making connections to promote employee engagement and make more of an impact.

In *The Tipping Point*, Malcolm Gladwell writes about how apparently little things can make a big difference. He uses the term "tipping point" to describe a big change that takes off as a result of something driven by an apparently small factor. Gladwell likens this type of change to epidemics or trends that spread widely. Examples include an unknown book becoming a best seller, a shoe becoming a fashion trend, or a crime rate dramatically dropping.

One of the factors that help things take off, or "tip," is a type of person Gladwell calls a "connector." Connectors have a "special gift" for making friends and acquaintances and bringing others together. They get to know many people partly because they have a foot in many different worlds over time, whether they be professions, community groups, or associations. They are respected by many and can influence big changes.

Gladwell cites the example of Paul Revere, whose midnight ride from Boston to Lexington to warn of British army plans to march to Lexington mobilized American colonists to fight. Gladwell also talks about a second midnight rider named William Dawes, who set out from

Boston at the same time as Paul Revere. Whereas Revere is now famous, Dawes is little known. Gladwell contrasts Revere's success in mobilizing the people with that of Dawes. In the years prior to his famous ride, Revere had drawn on his gregarious and social nature and ability to build relationships with many people. During his ride through the towns on the way to Lexington, he called on his many friends and acquaintances, who trusted him, listened, and acted. Dawes, in contrast, had nowhere near Revere's social connections with people in the communities he passed through, so he was nowhere near as effective in mobilizing the people.

After reading *The Tipping Point*, we realized that we could use the idea of connectors to help spread the transformation and engagement work we do. We identified connectors in our organization and asked that they help connect us with others in order to affect change.

Tribal Leadership, by Dave Logan, John King, and Halee Fischer-Wright, is the second book that taught us about the power of making connections. As we discuss elsewhere in our book and recap briefly here, *Tribal Leadership* discusses how humans naturally form into tribes. In organizations, tribes are where work gets done. Great tribal leaders are those who can connect members of their tribes with members of other tribes, bring them together, and inspire them to collaborate toward a common vision. These leaders don't make connections with a goal of increasing their own power; they make connections to enable people from the other tribes to collaborate to create something greater than themselves. They help the tribes move up the five levels of tribal cultures, from level 1 ("Life sucks.") to level 2 ("My life sucks.") to level 3 ("I'm great and you're not.") to level 4 ("We're great together."), and to the pinnacle, level 5, ("Life is great.")

where they are changing the world. As one moves into the top two levels of tribal culture, employee engagement soars.

In organizations, getting great results often requires getting multiple groups to form a collaborative relationship. One of the ways tribal leaders create engagement is by connecting two people to form a triad (the person making the connection is the third person in the triad). It's about forming three-legged relationships that bring the tribes together. When triads are formed across the organization, it enables the culture to shift from "we're great and you're not" to "we're great together." The leader could accomplish the shift by encouraging those people he or she connected to work together on a project or solve a problem. Additionally, just as tribal leaders can create triads among individuals, they can also create triads among groups such as departments, which can then collaborate more effectively.

A networking organization named Beacon taught us about helping others make connections. Beacon has a wonderful culture of people helping each other with career networking. Members help others who are between jobs or thinking about making a transition. They connect people with others in their field of interest and help them connect with hiring managers at companies where they've applied for positions. They also help early-career professionals get a foot in the door. It's incredibly gratifying to help others make connections and become uplifted and engaged as a result.

What you could do to promote engagement:
You don't have to be a strong connector or a leader to connect people. By introducing people across functions to accomplish a shared goal, you are also establishing a culture of collaboration. By connecting others, you also can increase your own impact and opportunities. You don't have to wait

for others to connect you. You can observe who the connectors are in your organization and ask some of them to introduce you to others with whom you might collaborate. Ultimately, engagement will increase.

12. Drive Out Fear

W. Edwards Deming, one of the most influential business and quality improvement educators of the 20th century, developed 14 management principles for significantly improving the effectiveness of an organization. One of these was focused on driving out fear. The point reads as follows:

> **Drive out fear:** *Encourage effective two-way communication and other means to drive out fear throughout the organization so that everybody may work effectively and more productively for the company.*

Deming understood the connection between people feeling secure and their willingness to fully contribute their talents and help the organization innovate and execute.

Job insecurity is one of the most obvious sources of fear. Many organizations create fear and resistance to change by the way they approach change. We have seen organizations launch process improvement initiatives that are quickly followed by layoffs. Sometimes that is management's intent from the start. This approach totally undermines process improvement efforts. If one believes that an organization needs to constantly and continually strive to improve its processes in order to survive and thrive, one needs people at all levels to own and support those efforts. However, when employees see colleagues getting laid off as a result, they become disengaged and learn to resist change.

Several companies stand out in their history for zero or minimal layoffs. These include Southwest Airlines, Toyota, Nucor, Lincoln Electric, FedEx, Aflac, and Erie Insurance.[9] Some of these companies have no-layoff policies, while others have avoided layoffs for decades. For example, Toyota, which until recently had never laid off employees, engages employees in training and process improvement during economic downturns. When they do make improvements, they do not eliminate those jobs. They redesign the jobs and reallocate personnel. As we mention elsewhere in the book, Pixar identified cost reduction as a key objective and deeply involved their entire workforce in coming up with ideas and ways to address this challenge. Executive leadership made clear from the outset that this effort was NOT designed to discover where they could cut staff.   The employees embraced the challenge and drove the changes.

Although the days of companies promising loyal employees lifetime employment are gone, some companies strive to offer their employees something that perhaps makes people feel similarly secure. They facilitate employees' becoming more employable than when they joined the company. These companies offer development opportunities that make employees more marketable. The resulting gratitude and reduced insecurity promote deeper engagement.

During recessions some companies find ways to reduce costs without resorting to layoffs. These include shorter work

---

[9] http://money.cnn.com/2008/12/09/news/economy/no_layoffs/

weeks at reduced pay, sabbaticals, longer year-end breaks, and reallocating employees to departments with more needs.

Economic downturns are also an opportunity to get good deals with suppliers while helping them avoid making layoffs. Some years ago we did some research for Anheuser-Busch into the benefits of making capital investments during a recession. Suppliers, who are grateful to get the work, are willing to be more competitive in their pricing. Plus, the investments Anheuser-Busch made while competitors were cutting back positioned it for growth when the economy eventually strengthened.

What you could do to promote engagement:
When process improvements make operations more efficient or effective, offer employees new opportunities rather than cutting jobs. Build for the long term rather than for short-term financial results. During hard times, be as creative as possible with managing costs vs. laying off staff.

13. Make People's Day Better

Our colleague Ronnette (Ronnie) Watson has a remarkable ability to make people feel comfortable and appreciated, and generally, make their day better. We recognized this skill as a great way to facilitate employee engagement. So for this chapter, we sat down with Ronnie to explore how she makes a person's day better and to understand how that effort promotes engagement.

So, Ronnie, please tell us about your approach.

Ronnie: Making someone's day better is a powerful lever for getting them engaged. It comes naturally to me, but I think anyone can learn to make people's day better. Generally, you need to:

- Make people feel comfortable.
- Embrace who the person is.
- Try to make people smile.
- Compliment people.
- Make people feel appreciated.
- Make people feel better about themselves.
- Help people build relationships.

- Give people a moment of serenity (amidst the anxiety in the world).
- Don't be so into yourself.
- Make things fun.

Can you please elaborate on how you accomplish each of these actions you recommend?

Make people feel comfortable.

Sometimes you can see in a person's face that they are uncomfortable or feel anxious around others, and I try to make them feel comfortable. Many people are uncomfortable meeting others for the first time. For example, I could tell a new employee was a little nervous so I asked, "How are you doing?" I welcomed her and told her that if there's anything she needs, she could come and see me and I could answer any questions she has and tell her more about what we do. I let her know that she could always come to me because I have an open door policy. I immediately saw the relief on her face. We have since become friends and business collaborators.

Embrace who the person is.

There is good in everybody. If someone seems difficult and unpleasant, you just have to bring the good out of them. There's a manager I know who is unnecessarily overbearing and controlling. But once you know that about a person, you can accept that personal characteristic. And when you do, that person will sometimes let you see another side of them. You need to get past that initial challenge. Difficult people may not want others to see the real them, and they may use a challenging facade as a defense mechanism. If you embrace who the person is, he or she may let their guard down and then you can build a relationship. It's okay that people are different. You need to embrace who they are and see if they can fit into your life. If not, just keep moving. But, when you are able to make the connection, you and the other person create a space for both of you to be more engaged.

Try to make people smile.

If I see someone in the hallway or elevator and they are not smiling, I smile and say, "Hey, how's your day?" Sometimes, though, I can't tell from their face. A person might be frowning even though they are not having a bad day. I might walk up to a person and say, "Aww, you're not having a good day?" and they look at me like "Who is this crazy person?" And I'll say, "Just smile, your day will get better." That will sometimes spark them to say, "You know what? You're right. I didn't even know I wasn't smiling because I'm actually really happy inside." We may run into each other later in the day, and as soon as they see my face they'll start smiling. I'll know it's because of what I said to them earlier.

Sometimes I'll see someone who appears stressed or is frowning, and I might say to them, "It can't be that bad. Someone else has it worse than you." Or, I might say, "What can I do to make you smile?" When we part, I might say, "I'm going to come back later and check on you." And the key is to really do it. So, I'll come back and say, "How was the rest of your day?" First, they're shocked to see me because they thought it was just something to say. And second, they think, "Wow, you really do care how my day was, it wasn't like you were just saying it in passing."

Make people feel appreciated.

If employees feel appreciated they'll give you their all. For example, I was working with a department that included a group of people whose jobs involve entering data. They believed others in the organization didn't value their efforts. So I pointed out to them that if they didn't get the data in there how would others be able to do their jobs? And I also let them know how much I appreciate them. When they hear me appreciate them and what they do, they respond, "Wow!" Once they asked, "Could you tell our boss that?" And, I did! Later that day I went to their boss and said, "You have really wonderful people working for you. Do you tell them you appreciate them?" She became quiet for a moment and then said, "Probably not as much as I should." I replied, "Why don't you do that? It makes them feel real good and you might get more out of them." Later that week, she went to each employee and told them how much she appreciated them.

The next time I asked a worker how her day was going, she told me, "You know, my manager came over and told me she appreciated what I'm doing." I asked her, "How did that make you feel?" And she replied, "Different, in a good way."

So my advice is that you go around and tell people how much you appreciate them and what they are doing, no matter how small or big a thing it is. You will notice that it actually makes *you* feel better to see the reaction on their faces.

Make people feel better about themselves.

When I see people in the elevator, I compliment them. For example, I'll say, "I like your tie because it matches your eyes," "You smell very nice today," or "Those shoes look good on you." I can't look at somebody and not have anything positive to say. It changes their body language and facial expressions. I can see the smile coming. Even if it doesn't happen then, it may the next time they see me. They just light up. They might not even say anything, but just smile. And that's cool with me. When I walk past and see you smile, I know. And I'm satisfied by that because I made you smile.

Help people build relationships.

In the workplace we collaborate with different departments. People are so used to working in silos, but our group works across departments. You don't realize how your job depends on theirs and theirs on yours until you get to know what they do. When we talk to others outside our immediate area and when we collaborate, things come together and make sense like one big completed puzzle put together from pieces that don't necessarily make sense by themselves.

I might be working on something and then feel the need to ask someone if I can bounce ideas off of them. They tell me what they do. And I say I didn't know you do that. I do try to make connections in order to help. I might say I know the manager in another department who might be a resource for you. I can introduce them to build a relationship and get things done. So instead of "spinning," they are able to get more done thanks to a new relationship.

Give people a moment of serenity (amidst the anxiety in the world).

Sometimes it will be obvious that someone is really stressed out. It might be the job; it might be something personal. I'll come over and talk about something other than what the person is going through. If I know the person and their interests, I gear my conversation toward that. For example, if I know someone enjoys gardening or horses I will start talking about that hobby. I'll even ask about what they are going to do for the weekend. I may mention a vacation I took with my grandkids or a vacation I want to take. This small talk gets their mind off of the immediate problem and into something more serene. Once I see that they are calming down I may throw in some suggestions about the topic that was bothering them and try to help them see the bright side. For me, there's always a brighter side.

Don't be so into yourself.

Don't be so into yourself. People are really, really self-focused. Their thinking is hard to describe, but it's something like, "I'm going to this meeting and it's about what I can do."

I recommend that you do the opposite. Don't even think about yourself. Think about the other people, who they are, and what might be important to them. I don't go in a meeting thinking about myself. I first look to see who's in the meeting and whether I know them. If I don't know them, those are the people I really want to get to know. When you focus on these people rather than yourself, you make their day better and you are probably going to be more successful over time getting things done because you are building relationships, not opposition.

Make things fun.

I'll use an example of making things fun. When I used to do training for a system, some people would resist because it was a new system and something else they had to learn. Others worried that their jobs were going away. Many basically didn't want to go to a training class, while others felt training was a complete waste of time. Sometimes, when I would go through the training topics I would notice reactions of boredom, distraction, and sleepiness on people's faces. So I'd start to say things to make them laugh. I might say, "What is that look on your face for? It's not that bad." Or I'd say something funny or silly. I'd even go off topic. I might tell a story about my grandson. I might tell them something about me. People love stories and funny stuff. By breaking the monotony of presentation with a good story, you reengage your audience and they are better able to focus on the presentation.

I also make things fun in general. Sometimes I make fun of what we're doing. I try to make people laugh. As I mentioned, if I walk past someone who seems like they aren't having a good day, I say something to make them smile or laugh.

Any parting thoughts, Ronnie?

Yes, I have a few more things I'd like to share.

I'm confused by the fact that more people don't do what I do. Anybody can do the things I talked about. It just takes a little practice.

It's such an awesome feeling to talk to people, and for them to come see you, even if you're not really a people person. I know plenty of people who are not people persons. They won't smile no matter what I say. But, I don't give up because my attitude is even if you don't smile and you don't speak to me, I'm still going to say hi to you. One day you're going to walk in here and you're going to say hi or you're going to smile and I'm going to have a "gotcha" moment.

These efforts to connect with people could also be done at the executive level. For example, you could suggest that the CEO come around every so often and say hello and thank you to the workers. On Halloween or Valentine's Day she or he could walk around giving out candy. Or, every once in a while they could stand by the front door for a half hour, greeting employees and handing them a food item as they come into work.

Can you imagine the impact of the CEO standing by the door greeting you in the morning? Wow! The buzz would go around the organization. People would say, "Did you know the CEO was standing at the door this morning saying 'Hi' and 'Have a good day'?"

You would be surprised how the slightest little thing makes somebody's day. If the CEO greeted me, I would tell the CEO to have an even better day, and make an impact on him.

Last but not least, you want to combine being productive with having fun. If you have fun while being productive, you will be into it, the results will mean something to you, and you will do it well. If you are not having fun and it is something you are told you must do, you are more likely to do just enough to get by.

14. Be More of a Giver than a Taker

"If you pick up a starving dog and make him prosperous he will not bite you. This is the principal difference between a dog and man."

Mark Twain

"You can easily judge the character of others by how they treat those who can do nothing for them or to them."

Malcolm Forbes

This is a short chapter but one with an impactful message: Being a "giver" to others can be a powerful lever for engagement. Our longtime colleague and friend Gregg Brandyberry has a big heart and likes to say, "There are givers and takers in this world." Gregg has helped so many people become more successful in their careers. He has gotten people assigned to desirable projects, recommended them for promotions, coached and mentored, and taken chances placing them in new roles.

Earlier in our careers we were helped by several generous colleagues and mentors. Some took us under their wing. Some gave us jobs and project opportunities. Some gave us emotional support and wise counsel to get through difficult situations. As a result we became so much more committed to and productive in our work.

Partly due to others' generosity in assisting us, we have tried to be generous in helping people starting out in their careers as well as those who are already established. We have noticed that some people are grateful for the help others have given them and they actually reciprocate even though it is not expected. We have also have seen others turn their backs on those who have helped them substantially. That doesn't stop us.

You are a giver when you:

- Include someone in a project.
- Give someone a chance to do something new.
- Connect someone with another person who can help them.

Givers are happier than takers because it feels good to give. We have done countless interviews where we ask people about the pleasures of their job. The number one response from nurses, scientists, lawyers, teachers, doctors, and managers is that they make a difference in others' lives.

Helping is contagious. It sets a good example for others to follow, fostering a culture of collaboration, which leads to further engagement.

Even if you are early in your career, you can still give. For example, you could help a graduating student get an interview or pass their resume to a hiring manager.

Summarizing unhealthy practice -- Avoiding disengagement:

Ask yourself a few honest questions. Do you take more than you give? Do you show respect, return giving, and express gratitude to those who have gone out of their way to help you in a meaningful way? If the answer is no, you are probably being a taker. Fortunately, you can start changing today.

What you could do to promote engagement:

If you're not already going out of your way to help others around you, begin doing more today.

Part IV

Human Motivation

15. Improve Quality of Work Life

A management movement called quality of work life (QWL) emerged in the 1970s. This movement was influenced by the thinking of people such as Abraham Maslow, an American psychologist who developed his famous hierarchy of needs in the 1940s.

The QWL movement identified a number of ways to increase the satisfaction people derive from their work. The auto industry provides a good example. The moving auto assembly line, launched by Henry Ford in 1913, had divided work into small, simple tasks that required little training. It was incredibly efficient, but mind-numbingly boring and dehumanizing, despite the relatively high wages. To better engage their employees, companies such as Volvo redesigned the way they built cars in the 1970s. Volvo made small teams responsible for the manufacture of an entire car, enriching the automakers' work through cross training, job rotations, autonomy, and personal and skill development, among others.

Russell Ackoff, an American organizational theorist, management educator, and Anheuser-Busch Professor Emeritus of Management Science at the Wharton School, University of Pennsylvania, and others extended QWL concepts by advocating for and implementing programs where employees were given a voice into how their quality of work life could be improved. In one example, Ackoff worked with Alcoa's aluminum products manufacturing facility in Tennessee. When he arrived, management and union relations were antagonistic to the point of violence, quality and productivity were the lowest in the network, and the plant had been slated for closure by Corporate. By the time Ackoff finished the engagement, corporate decided to keep the plant open and to invest $500 million in modernization. In time, the plant achieved the highest productivity in the network. How did they do that?

Alcoa started a quality of work life program. Ackoff advised management to start by meeting with union members and asking what could be done to improve the quality of work life. Labor made numerous suggestions, and although some were minor, quick action by management helped rebuild trust, which then enabled bigger improvements. For example, employees complained that their cafeteria was run down while the executive cafeteria was lavish. They were also resentful that managers had designated parking spots and they didn't. They said that management didn't listen to their ideas. Under Ackoff's tutelage, management immediately made all parking spots "first come, first served." They closed the executive dining room and created a single, updated cafeteria.

The goodwill created by these and other changes improved morale and trust and led to a process for labor to submit ideas to improve the business. For example, a veteran worker suggested installing rubber mats at the end of the production line so that rolls of aluminum would not become dented – and thus defective. This idea saved the company $25 million per year!

When Ackoff heard about this improvement, he privately asked the worker how long he had known rubber mats would result in a cost savings. The worker sheepishly looked down at his feet in silence. Ackoff prodded, "C'mon, I won't say a word to management." Still looking down, the worker murmured, "25 years."

"Why didn't you say anything sooner?" Ackoff asked. The laborer looked him in the eye and said, "The sons of bitches never asked me."

Wow! Imagine if this employee had been engaged years earlier! Imagine what ideas the employees in your organization are waiting to share!

In another of Russ' stories about the need for a quality of work-life program, a customer who had bought a Cadillac drove it off the lot and returned a few minutes later, complaining of a rattling noise in the driver-side door. The dealer looked over the door and found nothing obviously wrong. The customer left with the car, but returned the next day and handed over the keys, saying he wouldn't take the car back until it was fixed. Only when the mechanic disassembled the door did he find the problem – a coke bottle in the bottom of the door! He saw a piece of paper inside the bottle and coaxed it out. On it was a note that read, "Congratulations – You bastards finally found it!" We can only imagine what may have motivated the employee to write this note.

Summarizing unhealthy practice -- Avoiding disengagement:

If you're not asking your employees what you can do to improve their quality of work life, you are missing an important opportunity to simultaneously improve both quality and employee engagement. However, if you start a QWL program, be prepared to follow through on some of the

....

ideas. Otherwise, employees could become even more disengaged.

What you could do to promote engagement:

Ackoff used to say, "If you want to improve quality, don't start by focusing directly on improving quality; instead, start by focusing on improving quality of work life, and your employees will give you quality."

If your organization does not have a program to improve the quality of work life, we recommend starting one. Fairly easy to start, these programs are a great way to improve employee engagement because they offer employees an opportunity to express ideas. You can set up sessions where employees get together to come up with suggestions. As usual, make it clear that ideas generated will need to be reviewed to determine which are doable, and make sure to follow through with explanations for those which cannot be done. You could have executives come to a town hall to say what can be done, what cannot be done, and what needs to be further evaluated. For the latter, management should commit to providing answers within a month or so.

Another variation of improving quality of work-life is for a manager to meet with her subordinates to ask how she can help them do their jobs better. Subordinates should be instructed to stay positive and suggest ways the manager could help them do their jobs better. The discussion should not devolve into what the manager is doing wrong. This tactic can be powerful because it reveals ideas that would be easy for the manager to implement.

16. Tap into Human Motivation

"If I accept you as you are, I will make you worse; however, if I treat you as though you are what you are capable of becoming, I help you become that."

Johann Wolfgang von Goethe

"Everybody's looking for someplace to be somebody."
Herman Wrice

It's human nature to want to make a difference, to learn and continually improve, and make a difference for others. This intrinsic motivation is hard wired. The best organizations know how to tap into and actualize this motivation. Unfortunately, most organizations, intentionally or unintentionally, tamp it down.

Fortunately, there's a lot we can do. Fields including psychology and neuroscience provide insights into motivation. Kent Berridge, a neuroscientist at the University of Michigan, has done pioneering research into pleasure and desire. He found that the part of the brain that lights up when we enjoy something is the same for accomplishment, food, sex, shopping, being smiled at, drugs, and money. However, this pleasure is fleeting, and humans have an always-on desire, wanting to get to the next level. This reward system, according to a 2015 article in *Intelligent Life* magazine, propels us to constantly seek out what we need. It explains that the nature of desire is never to reach permanent satisfaction. One always strives for the next thing.[10]

If humans are "insatiable wanting machines," as the article suggests, then there are major implications for cultivating an engaged workforce. Employees who feel the pleasure of continuing accomplishment, recognition, mastery, and purpose at work, are more likely to become engaged, partly because the reward centers of their brain are activated. To the extent they feel they cannot achieve their needs and wants at work, they will channel their energies and engagement elsewhere. We believe this is quite prevalent.

To provide some historical context, let's step back more than 75 years to examine the work of Viktor Frankl, who was one of the most prominent psychiatrists of the 20th century. Frankl survived Nazi concentration camps in World War II, founded the field of logotherapy, and wrote about both in *Man's Search for Meaning*. He vividly describes how some people in the concentration camps were able to stay focused on some purpose, whether present or future, while others lost their sense of meaning and purpose, and gave up. After the war Frankl founded logotherapy, to help people find purpose or meaning in their lives. Patients undergoing logotherapy experienced fewer problems such as depression, aggression, and addiction. Frankl and his followers believe

---

[10] http://moreintelligentlife.com/content/features/wanting-versus-liking?page=full#_

that the search for meaning is the primary driver in life. This proposition has fascinating implications for many facets of society. In organizations, it suggests that focusing on making people happy is less likely to promote engagement (!) than focusing on creating an environment wherein employees can find meaning or purpose.

Frankl also says that if you strive hard for something, you are less likely to achieve it than if you focus on meaning. For example, if you focus explicitly on pursuing happiness, you will not likely achieve it, and you will be disappointed because it's fleeting. If, instead, you focus on adding meaning or purpose in your life, happiness could be a byproduct of that focus. On a societal level, it suggests that "the pursuit of happiness," as outlined in the U.S. constitution, might have been better focused on the pursuit of meaning or purpose (which is quite compatible with business success). No doubt that when Thomas Jefferson penned the phrase "life, liberty, and the pursuit of happiness" in the Declaration of Independence, he was aware of the teachings and writings of the Greek Epicurus and the Roman Lucretius. Both ancient philosophers advocated for the pursuit of pleasure, but not in the sense you might be thinking. Their concept of pleasure derived from the satisfaction from doing good things for others.

Another 20th century pioneer, Frederick Herzberg, the psychology and management thinker (and originator of "job enrichment" at AT&T), studied job satisfaction and dissatisfaction. Herzberg wrote one of *Harvard Business Review*'s most requested articles, "One More Time: How do You Motivate Employees?" [11] In this article, Herzberg

---

[11] Herzberg, Frederick. *Harvard Business Review*. January-February 1968.

concluded that money is not a motivator. Insufficient money could be a demotivator, but contrary to what some might expect, giving more and more money as a reward is not an effective motivator. Rather, people are much more motivated by making an impact, being recognized, or being appreciated. This conclusion is consistent with Frankl's insights on finding a sense of meaning as the primary driver for motivation. According to Herzberg, money is more of a transitory pleasure. Sure, we're excited if we receive a big bonus or get a new car, but that soon wears off, and we anticipate our next "fix." More lasting is the sense that you are making a difference for others. Our personal experience bears this out. We interviewed 55 people in a pharmaceuticals development and manufacturing organization, and when asked what they wanted from their job, the number one response was "to make a difference for others [in my little part of the world]."

Chip Conley, twenty-first century hotelier, hospitality entrepreneur, and author, has applied motivation concepts from psychologist Abraham Maslow, resulting in a highly engaged workforce. He founded Joie de Vivre, a hotel, spa, and restaurant business, where he applied the concepts from Maslow's hierarchy of needs. Maslow's hierarchy places base needs such as survival (food, shelter, money, safety) at the bottom of a pyramid, and puts higher-level needs such as love/belonging, self-esteem, and self-actualization in the higher levels of the pyramid.

Conley created a virtuous, reinforcing circle in which all levels of the pyramid interact to foster strong engagement. In this model, an organization creates a unique corporate culture and vision that leads to enthusiastic staff. The staff then satisfy unmet customer needs, leading to strong customer loyalty and a profitable, sustainable business.

Here's an illustrative example from Conley's book, *Peak: How Great Companies Get Their Mojo from Maslow*. The company came up with a vision for a Rock 'n Roll hotel experience in which the mission was to create a unique experience for traveling rock bands, musicians, and filmmakers. The unique artifacts and sense of community fulfilled what was missing from "box" hotels where the rooms are similar and there is often little or no community. Conley discusses the huge influence on customers' experiences of relatively-low-paid cleaners and front desk staff who became highly engaged when they saw their work in the context of creating an exciting, unique experience for the guests. The efforts made by these employees is similar to that of the extraordinary guest experience employees (known as "cast members") provide at Disney resorts. At Joie de Vivre, a bathroom cleaner no longer just had a job to do; their work was a key part of the most extraordinary guest experience.

Daniel Pink, in his 2011 book *Drive*, discusses mistakes many people make when trying to motivate others. They assume that external rewards such as money, punishments, and performance goals or grades will motivate employees, but Pink indicates these rewards may be effective in only very limited circumstances, and often create unintended consequences. In fact, extrinsic rewards usually demotivate. Twenty-first century organizations require creative, engaged people for success. However, extrinsic motivators tend to shunt creativity and discretionary effort. External rewards often take the joy out of activities that employees would otherwise happily do.

Pink makes a compelling case that humans are intrinsically motivated and that the way to motivate people is to allow their intrinsic motivation to be actualized. He highlights three main dimensions of motivation -- autonomy, mastery, and purpose. Autonomy fulfills our desire to direct our own lives; mastery is the process of getting better at an activity or skill -- learning and creating new things; and purpose is about doing better by ourselves and our world. He calls this Motivation 3.0 and advocates this intrinsic-motivation based model for the 21st century.

In contrast to Motivation 3.0, Pink identifies Motivation 1.0 as the basis for prehistoric man, and asserts that the focus was on the fight to survive. Pink also asserts that Motivation 2.0, which focuses mainly around rewards and punishments (aka, carrots and sticks), was the prevailing model as civilizations formed, and it has continued to prevail up until today.

We believe that Pink's assertions about Motivation 1.0 and 2.0 are in some ways oversimplified. For example, people living tens of thousands of years ago, and also in the last few millennia, were much like people today in terms of their desire to direct their own lives, learn, and make an impact. Although life expectancy was lower (a higher percentage died in childbirth and from disease, driving down average) those who survived took pride in their work as evidenced by the rich history of innovations in language, writing, mathematics, architecture, and farming. Nevertheless, we fully agree with Pink about how the Motivation 2.0 model, as applied in business and education over the past 150 years or so, has been counterproductive and dehumanizing, and has damaged employee and student engagement. Pink eloquently makes the case for the need for a new model that will enable intrinsic motivation to flourish.

Several companies provide examples of progress in Pink's autonomy dimension. And, these practices are not just about helping people actualize their autonomy. They are part of a strategy of creating an environment that leads to new revenue and profit streams. The classic example is 3M, which has a history of allowing its engineers to spend 15 percent of their time on work that they (intrinsically) want to pursue. The invention of Post-It Notes is one noteworthy (pun intended) outcome of this practice. Spencer Silver, an engineer, had accidentally created a glue that wasn't very strong and wouldn't dry. When he initially asked colleagues for ideas about how the glue might be used, no one had a suggestion. But his colleague Art Fry had aha moment one day when he dropped his choir hymnal in church and the paper bookmarks fell out. Fry realized that Silver's glue could be used to temporarily hold the paper in place. Eventually Silver and Fry got the chance to develop and market what would become a blockbuster product.

Google, perhaps inspired by 3M's example, has allowed employees to intrinsically pursue their own ideas for services. Google News is one such service. It was developed by Krishna Bharat, who had an interest in stories related to September 11, 2001. To provide more freedom to the business units offering the various products and services its employees have innovated, Google formed Alphabet, an umbrella company, in 2015.

Amazon's CEO Jeff Bezos is intently focused on creating and maintaining a culture that encourages, and actually drives, the pursuit of new business ideas as a way for the company to thrive. Amazon Web Services (AWS) is a remarkable example of the autonomy to innovate. Chris Pinkham, Benjamin Black, and others conceived of and built AWS, the fastest growing business segment and the largest source of Amazon's profits.

The Motivation 3.0 model is not only being practiced in corporations. Some educational institutions, nonprofits, and government agencies are applying it. One school is the

Sudbury Valley School, founded in Framingham, Massachusetts in 1968 to allow children's intrinsic motivations to drive their learning within a democratically run school. In these schools, children aged 4-19 are free from tests, required classes, schedules, and homework. They have both the freedom and the responsibility to decide how to spend their time, what they want to learn, what to do with others, and whether to get involved in managing the school. Studies have shown the graduates to be well-adjusted leaders and embracers of change. We have been fortunate to observe this type of learning environment first-hand, at the Philadelphia Free School, which is modeled after the Sudbury Valley School. The level of engagement is remarkable, and it is refreshing to see children's intrinsic motivations encouraged and supported. (If you would like to learn more about intrinsic motivation in education, we suggest that you read Dan Greenberg (cofounder of Sudbury Valley School) and Alfie Kohn (a recognized authority on the intrinsic nature of learning)).

Summarizing unhealthy practice -- Avoiding disengagement:

Dismantling much of the internally focused quotas and metrics will be helpful in addressing employee disengagement. Carrots and sticks — extrinsic motivators — rarely work. Tough talk about holding people accountable usually backfires and is a sign that something more fundamental needs to be fixed.

Narrowly focused metrics hurt employee morale and lead to poor customer service. Consider the following example. One back-office operation we know had quotas requiring each employee to complete at least 10 files per day, 50 per week. The manager regularly reported employees as nonperforming if they did not meet the quota. The manager also did not allow employees to talk with each other because he believed they would slack off. Three bad outcomes resulted. First, although completing the files required information that sometimes wasn't available from other departments, employees who pointed out issues were viewed as troublemakers. Thus, when information was missing, many employees would enter or attach information they knew was incorrect so they could meet the quota and stay out of trouble. (That sounds like a recipe for poor quality.) Second, when employees came across errors in the files, they hesitated to make corrections if it took away time from meeting the quota, so customer issues such as sending information to an incorrect address persisted. When a customer did not respond after three attempts (often due to notices being sent to the wrong address) their account sometimes would be closed out. Third, negative consequences rippled through the organization. Morale plummeted and employee absenteeism and medical leave soared.

Micromanaging how employees do their work hinders them from using their intrinsic motivation, creativity, and strengths to get results. Believing people are unmotivated can become a self-fulfilling prophecy. As a manager, don't forget that people need a feeling of relatedness, autonomy, opportunities for mastery, and a feeling of meaning and purpose.

What you could do to promote engagement:
Most people want to make an impact, do the right thing, and rise to expectations. In short, they are self-motivated. The key role for a manager is to create the space in which they can act on their intrinsic motivations.

Managers who have low expectations of their people or who feel the need to "hold their people accountable," should do some serious soul searching. Experiment with creating an environment where you encourage your people to create something great for their customers and the business. Become an enabler and *get out of the way!*

Part V

Empowering People

17. Become a Better Leader

"To lead people, walk beside them ... As for the best leaders, the people do not notice their existence. The next best, the people honor and praise. The next, the people fear; and the next, the people hate ... When the best leader's work is done the people say, 'We did it ourselves!'"

Lao Tsu

Leaders have a special responsibility and an opportunity to create an environment and culture that foster engagement. We have seen leaders whose style destroys engagement. On the lower extreme, some are sociopaths who see their subordinates as expendable resources. These leaders simply want to further their own goals, including maximizing their own quality of work-life at the expense of others. On the other end, we've seen leaders whose reason for being is to foster engagement, inspiration, development, and passion for achieving something great. In between, we see behaviors that foster various levels of commitment and engagement to the manager and/or the business.

We start this chapter with the concept of servant leadership. Robert Greenleaf, who worked at AT&T until

....

1964, coined the term "servant leader" in a 1970 essay. Greenleaf developed the idea after reading a novel by Herman Hesse:

> *The idea of The Servant as Leader came out of reading Hermann Hesse's Journey to the East. In this story we see a band of men on a mythical journey, probably also Hesse's own journey. The central figure of the story is Leo who accompanies the party as the servant who does their menial chores, but who also sustains them with his spirit and his song. He is a person of extraordinary presence. All goes well until Leo disappears. Then the group falls into disarray and the journey is abandoned. They cannot make it without the servant Leo. The narrator, one of the party, after some years of wandering finds Leo and is taken into the Order that had sponsored the journey. There he discovers that Leo, whom he had known first as servant, was in fact the titular head of the Order, its guiding spirit, a great and noble leader.[12]*

Greenleaf concludes that people should strive to be servants first, as Leo was. In other words, the best leaders emerge from servanthood rather than seeking to be leaders first. The servant takes care of other people's needs: their growth and development, their health, their wisdom, their ability to themselves become servants, and their willingness and ability to serve the least privileged in society.

---

[12] *The Servant as Leader.* Greenleaf, Robert K. 1970.
http://www.benning.army.mil/infantry/199th/OCS/content/pdf/The%20Servant%20as%20Leader.pdf

The servant leader sees himself or herself as at the bottom of an inverted pyramid, with the role of empowering their team to make a difference.

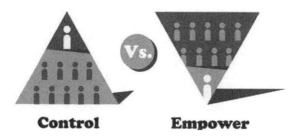

Control   **Empower**

Additionally, Greenleaf says that a new principle is emerging under which the only allegiance of the led to the leader is that which is "freely and knowingly granted" in relation to the servant stature and trust of the leader. In other words, the legitimacy of the leader depends on the willingness of people to follow her or him. This is consistent with some new forms of organization that have emerged in recent decades wherein employees do not report to a manager, and are free to choose what they work on. This is discussed in more detail in another chapter.

We view the role of servant leaders as a supporting one. Their mission is to help people achieve their objectives, become more capable and motivated (development), be successful, and be disciplined about working through challenges. Such leaders gain power by creating environments that enable others to be powerful.

Another source of insight is John Maxwell's *Five Levels of Leadership*. This book suggests ways managers can improve employee engagement through stronger leadership. Maxwell views leadership as influence. He reasons that if one person (a manager, for example) can influence others by gaining their respect, that manager can increase her or his influence on subordinates to achieve. Those subordinates can then help others succeed. It seems to us that influence could be a lever for engagement for both the leader and the followers because it could be encouraging and empowering for both.

Maxwell describes a five-level hierarchy of increasing influence (from 1 to 5), with each subsequent level including the levels below it. These levels are elaborated on below.

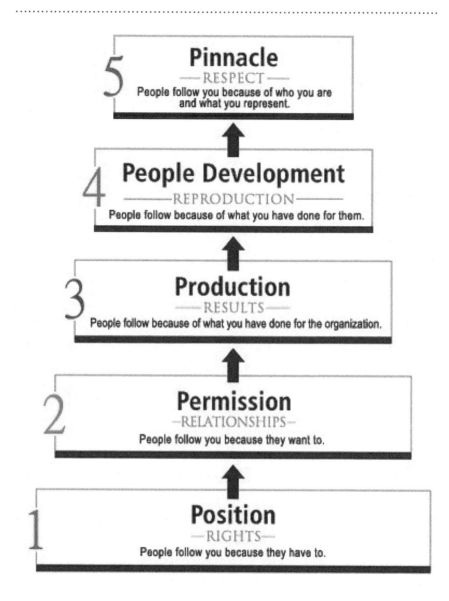

Level 1. When managers take a new role, they start out at level 1, the bottom level, where their basis for authority is the position. At this level subordinates follow the leader, at least to some extent, because they have to, but it is not the level at which leaders generate widespread and strong

commitment, nor is it where you are likely to find the most engaged employees.

Level 2. In level 1 employees follow managers because they have to. At level 2, they follow leaders because they want to. In other words, they give you "permission" to lead based on building two-way trust and solid, lasting relationships. In this scenario, employees get along better. More people like each other and the working environment is pleasant.

Level 3. Permission and a pleasant working environment are important, but to reach the next level a leader and her or his team need to be productive and get results. Influence is enhanced based on credibility from delivering results for the organization. At this level, morale and engagement may increase along with achieving goals, and improving revenues and profits. Level 3 gives leaders more opportunities to become change agents and to tackle more challenging problems. However, to become great, they must care about more than just their own results.

Level 4. At Level 4, a manager goes beyond his or her own results. At this level a leader helps others develop and become successful leaders in their own right. Because employees are aware of what the leader is doing for them personally, deeper relationships and loyalty are further built, and teamwork allows everyone's performance to improve. Followers see that the leader is genuinely interested in them and their success. In our experience, this is where engagement can really take off.

Level 5. This highest level leader helps others to develop into level 4 leaders. It is much more difficult and time consuming to develop leaders than to lead followers. These leaders create a legacy in what they do. Maxwell says that people follow them because of "who they are and what they represent."

Maxwell's levels 4 and 5 share some similarities with the servant leadership concept mentioned earlier. At these levels, leaders transcend themselves and "bring others with them." Subordinates see that the leader is about something bigger than themselves. They understand that the leader is making a space for them to create something great. This understanding fosters others to become leaders and it generates extraordinary engagement.

At which level of Maxwell's framework do you believe you are leading? You could make a substantial impact on engagement if you can move up in the levels.

We end this chapter with a third perspective, an excerpt from Ackoff's view on transformational leadership in which he contrasts administration with management:

> "These terms are often used interchangeably. What a waste! There are important differences they can be used to reveal. Therefore, I have defined them in a way that is directed at improving leadership and bringing about more significant organizational transformations.
>
> *Administration* consists of directing others in carrying out the will of a third party, using means selected by the same party.
>
> *Management* consists of directing others in the pursuit of ends using means, both of which have been selected by the manager. (Executives are managers who manage other managers.)

>*Leadership* consists of guiding, encouraging and facilitating the pursuit by others of ends using means, both of which they have either selected, or the selection of which they approve.

In this formulation, leadership requires an ability to bring the will of followers into consonance with that of the leader so they follow him or her *voluntarily*, with enthusiasm and dedication. Such voluntarism, enthusiasm, and dedication are not necessarily involved in either management or administration.

... a transformational leader is one who can formulate or facilitate the formulation of an inspiring vision of something to be sought even if it is unattainable, although it must at least be approachable without limit. The leader must also be able to encourage and facilitate (inspire) pursuit of the vision, by invoking the courage required to do so even when short-term sacrifices are required, by making that pursuit satisfying, fun as well as fulfilling."[13]

Summarizing unhealthy practice -- Avoiding disengagement:

Since servant leadership and leadership as influence and inspiration are personal, this section consists of a series of questions to help you assess your leadership for potential correction:

_____

[13] Ackoff, Russell L. *A Systemic View of Transformational Leadership*. http://www.acasa.upenn.edu/leadership.pdf

- Do you find yourself primarily focused on your own career success or that of only a small circle around you?
- Does something feel missing in terms of your life's work not being truly focused on making the lives of your consumers or constituencies better in some way?
- Is your minimal focus on serving subordinates creating a culture in which bad behavior flourishes?
- Are you pursuing short term results rather than an inspiring vision of an impact you and others could make in the company, industry, or world?

What you could do to promote engagement:
Following the advice and teachings of Greenleaf, Maxwell, and Ackoff could produce a powerful force for both results and engagement. We recommend that you:

- Give people a major role in shaping their work — both the ends and the means.
- Co-create an inspiring longer-term transformative vision for which people are willing to make short-term sacrifices.
- Serve your subordinates and other business partners by encouraging, facilitating, and guiding their pursuits.
- Try explicitly to nurture others to become leaders.
- View yourself as at the bottom of an inverted pyramid.

18. Listen to Your Employees

We have worked with many companies on process improvement, transformation, strategy, and visioning, but we think of ourselves as management educators/practitioners rather than as consultants. Consultants sometimes present external trends or best practices; sometimes they interview employees or other stakeholders. Then they often develop recommendations such as a new way to organize or a new strategy. When the consultants leave, the implementation of the recommendations largely depends on the employees and how "bought into" the recommendations they are. In contrast, we believe the strategy development/solution development/design process is inextricably tied to the execution process. This is how one gets buy-in to the strategy and its ultimate execution. Solving problems and delivering sustainable business results require employee buy-in and ownership of the issue. Employees must be part of designing the solution, and then implementing and embedding it.

The classic example of failure to involve employees is that thick report of consultant recommendations gathering dust on the shelf. But an unused report can be less damaging than employing the consultant's recommendations to push lower level employees to execute the strategy. Top-level executives, who are often disconnected from the realities and nuances of the day-to-day challenges and opportunities of the front-line functions, can lose their employees' faith when they push for solutions that those at lower levels believe are flawed. This situation occurred at a pharmaceutical company when the head of its R&D division used a high-profile consulting firm to develop a new structure and strategy for the organization. This restructuring, and a slew of previous restructurings dashed the morale of many scientists, and the head of R&D complained that people were not supporting the strategy. He expected them to adopt it by dictate. Sadly, the organization's development of new medicines was not enough to sustain the organization, and it continued to lay off workers.

It's not unusual for executive teams to huddle in a retreat to develop strategy. Some middle managers also fall into this trap, believing they have the all answers and that the "less intelligent" or "less aware" employees should fall into line. This behavior usually backfires, wasting time and resources and driving down morale.

We believe that all levels of employees should be deeply engaged in offering ideas and designing solutions because it leads to development opportunities, improved quality of work life, and of course, enhanced engagement. Again, we turn to Ackoff, who defined development as an increase in one's ability and desire to satisfy their legitimate needs and desires and those of others. People can develop when they are given multiple opportunities to fail, and thus learn from failures, becoming more capable over time. This may be the most important reason to engage your employees. They will learn and become leaders in their own right. Employees often complain about decisions made by higher-level managers. Involving those employees in such decisions provides an opportunity to gain their engagement.

Summarizing unhealthy practice -- Avoiding disengagement:

A manager who involves only a small number of people in making decisions likely will experience difficulty with implementation because employees not involved in the process will become disengaged.

What you could do to promote engagement:

Imagine if a CEO or other senior executive were to announce a new approach wherein the strategy and plans would now be influenced by or be based on ideas submitted from employees at all levels of the organization. To voice their ideas, employees could participate in person and submit ideas electronically. These submissions could even be voted on by other employees as a way to help filter those with the most appeal.

You don't need to be an executive to apply these concepts of listening to employees. Whether or not you manage people, you can start by seeking input and ideas from your colleagues. It's a proven way to build support and cut down on failing strategies.

19. Facilitate the Development of People

"Give a man a fish and you feed him for a day. Teach a man to fish and you feed him for a lifetime."

Ancient Chinese Proverb

Russell Ackoff defines development as an increase in one's ability and desire to satisfy their legitimate needs and desires and those of others. We believe that a focus on development is another effective way to enhance employee (or community) engagement.

Ackoff and his colleague, Jamshid Gharajedaghi, thought deeply about creating environments where development can blossom. Ackoff, who was educated in philosophy, reached back to his roots in Greek philosophy and identified four dimensions of development. Gharajedaghi identified a fifth. They both assert that development can be supported if progress can be made in these five dimensions:

1. Political (Power)
2. Aesthetics (Beauty/Vision/Inspiration/Excitement)
3. Knowledge/Wisdom (Truth)
4. Wealth (Resources/Efficiency)
5. Values (the Ethical-Moral)

Ackoff and Gharajedaghi then related these categories to the work of 18th century German philosopher Georg Wilhelm Friedrich Hegel. Hegel's insight was that one could integrate seemingly opposing or contradictory ideas so that both could be achieved. Now known as the Hegelian Dialectic, it articulates the view that sometimes you don't have to choose either this or that; sometimes you can have both.

In a very practical and powerful way, Ackoff and Gharajedaghi applied Hegel's ideas to the dimensions identified by the Greek philosophers. For example, Gharajedaghi was once working with an engineering firm client that created new equipment designs by passing draft designs from one engineering specialty to another (e.g., electrical to mechanical engineering). Unfortunately, it took a long time to get proposals back to clients using this process because there were inevitably delays and rerouting for rework. Gharajedaghi suggested that the client cross-train its engineers and have them work in cross-specialty groups to come up with the design. He said it could reduce the cycle time of the design process from six months to six weeks. Gharajedaghi focused on two of the dimensions — knowledge and wealth. He pointed out that if one person shares their knowledge with another, they have not lost it, they have duplicated it. He proposed that each of the engineering specialties would share their knowledge with the others. He also proposed that those who taught each other would receive bonuses. These people would then work in their cross-specialty groups to jointly develop a design. This process resulted in a quicker, more efficient response to customers and led to higher sales and profitability. The outcomes included higher pay for employees, enhanced knowledge, higher work satisfaction, satisfied clients, and higher employee engagement.

Rethinking the political dimension is quite promising as well. Ackoff and Gharajedaghi point out that if one rethinks power, one can become more powerful and effective. A manager might believe that her power over a team would decrease if others get more power. "Old-school" managers see themselves as having earned their way up higher in the pyramid, and they flex their power muscles over others. This type of manager may act as a "decision hog." He or she often allows only a few people to give input into key decisions in the area they manage.

As we discuss in detail elsewhere in this book, if we re-conceptualize power from "power over" to "power to do," a manager could actually increase her own power dramatically if she increases the power of her team to accomplish goals. Her team's success reflects positively on her. It's actually quite easy to start the shift to "power to do." You can talk with your team and ask them what they would like you to do to make it easier for them to do their jobs.

Aesthetics can also be an immensely effective dimension for promoting development. When people become inspired and excited by their accomplishments or what others have accomplished, they can make magnificent exertions. We are inspired, for example, by the great European cathedrals such as Notre Dame, Chartres, St. Peter's Basilica, and Florence's Duomo. Imagine the awe, pride, and commitment of the people who built these! This type of awe and commitment is sorely needed in today's organizations.

One of the inspirational examples of modern times is the 1960's U.S. space program whose mission was to get man onto the moon and back safely. The people involved in the program were enthralled with their work, which captured the

....

world's imagination and inspired countless people to do great things in other aspects of life. This is something that, unfortunately, is missing in most organizations. Many organizations focus on cost cutting, efficiencies, holding people accountable, and rolling out euphemistically-named programs (Operational Excellence, for example) that end up creating disengagement because they are actually justifications for layoffs.

Finally, we get to the values (ethical-moral) dimension of development. A key concept is "dissolving conflict," which involves redesigning something such as a product, a political process, or a strategy so that all conflicting parties get something they want.

When designing your ideal product, strategy or system, there is a tendency to move away from smaller objectives that conflict with your ability to accomplish multiple big-picture items at once. Suppose, for example, your organization is building a system that enables your customers to update their own information. By including information security and compliance groups in the up-front design process, their concerns will be addressed at the outset, avoiding internal conflict that could derail your project.

What you could do to promote engagement:
The five dimensions for development are conceptual, but you can take a number of concrete actions to facilitate progress. As discussed elsewhere in this book, they include using idealized design, developing visions, creating core values, and connecting people. Another way to foster development is to change your mindset, or "worldview," and that of others. Albert Einstein once said, "We can't solve problems by using the same kind of thinking we used when we created them."

One example of a different pattern of thinking that could produce breakthroughs and enhance engagement is to change our objective from "gaining power over others" to "making more of an impact by empowering others." Another would be to shift from "hoarding our knowledge" to "duplicating our knowledge to others."

Another way to promote development while re-engaging employees would be to let them share in creating something truly inspiring. Both the idealized design approach founded at Bell Laboratories and the visioning approach used at Zingerman's to inspire its employees and customers can be great ways to begin. At Griffin Hospital in Connecticut, the intense focus on allowing every employee to create an extraordinary patient experience supercharged their energy level and commitment. The retailer Nordstrom is another fertile example. Nordstrom encourages employees to use their best judgment in how they treat customers, in how they treat each other, and in how they conduct business ethically. This engages and empowers employees to come up with creative solutions that foster an extraordinary customer experience.

If you involve everybody in the organization, you can increase everyone's power (not giving up yours), which duplicates knowledge and increases energy levels. We like to think of it as having a giant copy machine that increases all development dimensions, leading to high engagement.

Part VI

Freedom and Accountability

20. Allow Employee Autonomy

"Control leads to compliance; autonomy leads to engagement."

Daniel H. Pink

In the second half of the 20th century, a movement emerged to bring more autonomy into the workplace. The prevalent model in most companies still tends more toward command and control, but this is changing. The new model fosters freedom and accountability.

Some companies provide employees with a lot of autonomy to operate within the purposes of the organization. One such company is Metalex, an advanced technology contract machining company. It specializes in the design, engineering, programming, fabrication, manufacture and inspection of complex, close tolerance parts, assemblies and tooling. Metalex posts projects and encourages employees to sign up to work on them, effectively allowing employees to choose their projects. This process provides learning opportunities and high job satisfaction. With the company's activity-based-costing system, the process enables people to track their effort and manage project costs. Here's what

Metalex says about its system for a self-directed workforce and about its people:

> *Metalex' nearly 40 years of ongoing success is based not only on strong relationships with its customers but also on the work ethic and performance of our people. Metalex has a self-directed workforce. Our employees refer to Metalex as "our" company because it's a team environment in which our people work and thrive.*
>
> *Each teammate has the opportunity to be the best they can be. Apprentice programs, ongoing education, a culture of knowledge sharing and our business model, Interaction Without Boundaries,™ which provides total clarity as to expectations from teammate to teammate, constantly raise job performance and personal fulfillment. As a result, Metalex has a team of exceptional, motivated teammates who take enormous pride in their contribution to each customer's success.*
>
> *Thanks to the talent and winning attitudes of our teammates, we are able to take on projects others deem too difficult and, regardless of tolerances and timelines, complete them on schedule.[14]*

There are many variations on employee autonomy, and the transition from a top-down controlled hierarchy is typically difficult. So, these transitions are not for the faint of heart.

---

[14] http://www.metalexmfg.com/our_people.html

At California-based Morning Star, the largest tomato processor in the world, employees are called "colleagues," and they have no managers. They have autonomy to do what they believe adds value to the organization. This autonomy does not lead to chaos because the freedom is balanced by responsibility. To balance autonomy and ensure accountability, compensation at Morning Star is peer based via employee-elected compensation committees. Each colleague writes a personal mission statement that covers how he or she will contribute to the enterprise's goals. Each year they write a colleague letter of understanding (CLOU), demonstrating how their personal mission serves as a commitment to the colleagues most affected by their work. At the end of each year, they are evaluated by their CLOU colleagues. Structure and coordination of work are achieved through a web of commitments among employees. Details of how the Morning Star process works are covered in the December 2011 *Harvard Business Review* article by Gary Hamel titled "First, Let's Fire all the Managers."[15]

Zappos began implementing its version of a manager-less organization, holacracy, in 2013. Zappos CEO Tony Hsieh concluded that the company would not achieve its ambitions with the traditional manager-employee hierarchy (which has prevailed in the United States since the 1800s). In this model, employees do not have a boss and are not on a single team. They seek to be either a "lead link" or a "rep link" on "circles" that are organized hierarchically. A circle operates within the clear purpose and accountabilities identified by the broader circle of which it's a part. Employees can participate in more than one circle. They are free to change

---

[15] https://hbr.org/2011/12/first-lets-fire-all-the-managers

circles, and lead links can say if they do not want a person in their circle.

Zappos' transition has been accompanied by a large percentage of the workforce leaving the company, but Hsieh is committed to autonomy models and appears to be continually adapting the model based on experience. Time will tell how effective Zappos' transition will be.

Some companies do not go as far as Metalex, Morning Star, or Zappos, but do grant employees autonomy for a percentage of their work time. As discussed earlier, 3M allows its engineers to spend up to 15% of their time working on their own ideas. Other companies hold what is being called a "FedEx Day." In this arrangement, some or all employees in a company are periodically allowed to work on whatever they want, as long as they show what they came up with 24 hours later. The name, as you may have guessed, comes from delivering something the next day. Employers could introduce the practice by allowing a department or a team to try it, and then expanding the practice to more employees. Some companies start with FedEx days once a month or once a quarter. Some companies do it once a week, calling it FedEx Thursdays.

Summarizing unhealthy practice -- Avoiding disengagement:

Managers with a dimmer view of human nature believe that employees need to be tightly managed and watched in order to get the most out of them. Perhaps they believe a small percentage of people would take advantage of their colleagues and not make a full effort to contribute. The other side of that coin, however, is that productive employees suffer from the tight control managers put in place to manage low performers. A key benefit of the emerging autonomy model is that low performers do not have a place to hide. Peer-based evaluation and compensation processes can effectively manage those people. Additionally, it becomes clear who is not contributing because it is easy to observe who is not being utilized.

What you could do to promote engagement:

Creating an organization with employee autonomy requires a fundamentally different way of thinking, and setting it up will require hard work and learning and mistakes and working out conflicts. For organizations that have stuck with it, an autonomy model seems well worth the effort, both for the employee empowerment and development and for the organizations' ability to adapt and thrive. For those wanting to start on a much smaller scale, allowing employees to work on whatever they want is a good way to start experimenting with the idea, and it can lead to intense employee engagement.

21. Implement a Democratic Organization

Note: This chapter comes with a warning: *"The Surgeon General has determined that if you are risk averse, you should skip this chapter."* This chapter is for courageous leaders, not managers who want to maintain the status quo. We have no illusion that the ideas presented here will be widely embraced in our time, but we do believe that bold ideas such as these will separate the organizations that will survive and thrive from those that will fall by the wayside owing to their inability to adapt.

Benjamin Franklin was a strong believer in the common man. In the Pennsylvania colony's militia (which Franklin helped establish in 1748), he implemented a democratic organization in which the militiamen elected their officers rather than their officers being appointed by the governor or Crown. [16] Years later, during the formation of the U.S. Constitution, Franklin battled the privileged aristocracy to win strong voting rights for the "common people." Franklin also advocated for the U.S. Congress to be elected by the

---

[16] Isaacson, Walter. *Benjamin Franklin: An American Life*. Simon & Schuster. 2003. P. 125.

people rather than be chosen by state legislatures. Franklin eventually helped broker a compromise in which the House of Representatives would be popularly elected and the Senate would be chosen by the state legislatures.[17] (The selection of senators was later changed to popular election.)

More recently, management educator Russell Ackoff was one of the strongest advocates in the 20th century for democratically-run corporations and government agencies. In his book, *The Democratic Corporation*, he lays out a design for participation of employees across levels, and includes a provision for employees to vote for the removal of a manager from his or her position. The manager would not be terminated. His or her superior could find them another position within the company. Variations on Ackoff's design have been implemented in parts of organizations including GlaxoSmithKline, the U.S. Navy, and the White House Communications Agency.

There are robust examples of democratic organizations in education. For example, at Sudbury Valley School and others inspired by the model, such as Philly Free School, the staff are subject to elections each year in order to continue their employment for the following year. Elections and voting are run by a body called "School Meeting," whose overwhelming majority consists of students. Students essentially have the major role in deciding whether staff can serve. This process is key to ensuring the staff serves the students.

The democratic organization has huge potential for fostering employee engagement. When leaders have the respect and confidence of their subordinates, they want to

---

[17] Isaacson, Walter. *Benjamin Franklin: An American Life*. Simon & Schuster. 2003. Pp. 448-452.

take direction from them and support making an impact. When he or she does not have their confidence, these subordinates are likely to become disengaged and even passively aggressive, especially when they believe there is a better way to do things.

We can think of numerous examples from our own careers where organizations would have been better served by enabling subordinates to remove a manager from their position. In one situation, employees working on a highly regarded software project became disengaged when an ambitious new manager thought she knew better and created her own grand, but disconnected, vision for the software. She refused to listen to the subordinates' pleadings to change the approach, viewing it instead as resistance to *her* change. The manager eventually left the company, but only after millions of dollars were wasted and after making the employees and users suffer for nearly two years.

In another case, a new manager for a back-office operation believed that his subordinates should not be talking with each other because he thought talking meant not working. He required employees to stay at their desks and be quiet. He also regularly berated his supervisors. Many employees would sometimes cry on their way to work. Employee turnover was very high and it took a long time to fill open positions.

What you could do to promote engagement:
The democratic organization will not be widely embraced at first, and implementing it is not for the faint of heart. We do believe, however, that democratic organizations will be one of the major 21st century levers for organizations of all types to build highly engaged teams. Democratic organizations can be created in any type of concern including businesses,

government agencies, non-profits, schools, and volunteer groups. Details on creating a democratic organization can also be found in Ackoff's book, *Recreating the Corporation*.[18]

---

[18] Ackoff, Russell L. *Recreating the Corporation: A Design of Organizations for the 21st Century*. Oxford University Press. 1999.

Part VII

Stairway from Heaven

22. Create Visions

"A true leader is one who designs the cathedral and then shares the vision that inspires others to build it."

Jan Carlzon

"I come with great enthusiasm, but with small faith. For it is clear that these are two different things. Man would be badly off, indeed, if he were incapable of enthusiasm except for the things in which he has faith! Humanity would still be pursuing its existence in a hole in the ground; for everything that made it possible to emerge from the cave and the primeval jungle appeared in its first hour as a highly dubious undertaking. Nevertheless, man has been able to grow enthusiastic over his vision of these unconvincing enterprises. He has put himself to work for the sake of an idea, seeking by magnificent exertions to arrive at the incredible. And in the end, he has arrived there. Beyond all doubt it is one of the vital sources of man's power, to be thus able to kindle enthusiasm from the mere glimmer of something improbable, difficult, remote."[19]

Jose Ortega y Gasset

As Ortega y Gasset so wisely points out, humankind's opportunity to advance is supported by this capacity and tenacity to form and realize a vision. In modern times there are countless examples. Let's think about one for the moment: human flight.

Flying machines had been imagined during the Renaissance by Leonardo Da Vinci, and probably long before that. Over centuries many others tried to devise a flying machine, until finally on December 17, 1903, Wilbur and Orville Wright succeeded with the first powered flight. While their feat is remarkable, it was predicated on the visions achieved by others such as the conception and invention of the internal combustion engine. After the Wright brothers, a succession of visionaries, including Howard Hughes, improved flight engineering, making the first moon landing possible, just 66 years later in 1969.

People with vision contributed to several remarkable breakthroughs that made space flight possible: electric circuits/lights, batteries, transistors, computers, computer languages, calculus, cameras, integrated circuits, steel, plastics, glass, temperature control, clocks, and radio communications. Visions can, of course, also be highly engaging in civic life.

---

[19] Mission of the University

In the Declaration of Independence, Thomas Jefferson understood the power of painting a vision and inspiring others to share in that vision:

> *We hold these truths to be self-evident, that all men are created equal, that they are endowed by their Creator with certain unalienable rights, that among these are Life, Liberty and the pursuit of Happiness. — That to secure these rights, Governments are instituted among Men, deriving their just powers from the consent of the governed ...*

Employees can become excited about and committed to a vision that gives their life meaning and provides satisfaction. If the vision inspires them, they are often more willing to make short-term sacrifices to achieve the longer term vision. The challenge, inspiration, and meaning translate directly to engagement. Let's think about an illustrative example from history. Imagine a medieval laborer building a cathedral. He knows the grand significance of what he is building and that it may not even be completed during his lifetime. Yet, he is dedicated to the result. Now, think of someone who has been assigned to build a brick wall but is not told about the bigger picture. He doesn't know if the wall is part of a building or enclosure, or the purpose of the structure. Who do you think will go about his role with more gusto?

Fortunately, there are actionable steps organizations and employees can take to create an engaging vision. Some of the best modern-day companies have seized on this concept of vision. Zingerman's food business is an extraordinary example.

Zingerman's employees love their jobs and its customers rave about its products and services. This is no accident. Zingerman's CEO Ari Weinzweig has sought out great practices from around the world and put them into effect in his organization, including:

- Building a culture of great service
- Defining core values
- Dedicating itself to constantly getting better
- Appreciating its employees

One of the great practices Weinzweig put into effect is a special form of visioning. Zingerman's way of visioning was inspired by the work of the late social scientist Ronald Lippitt and is different from the way most other organizations do it. Zingerman's first chooses a date in the future. The date might be 2-10 years in the future, depending on what it is designing. For example, if management and employees are writing a vision for their entire company, the vision would have a longer timeframe; for a project, it would be shorter. As a vision is drafted, opportunities are provided for many employees to comment on it and shape it. Zingerman's then writes the vision in narrative form, describing it in the present tense as if it were already in place. By visualizing the outcomes in advance, people are willing to support the needed organizational alignment. Excitement builds around it.

Weinzweig's excellent article on visioning [20] in *Inc.* summarizes the eight-step process for developing a vision:

> Step 1: Choose the topic for which you are writing the vision.

> Step 2: Pick your timeframe. (usually up to two years for a process)

> Step 3: Make a list of "prouds" — things you are proud of accomplishing, as if they've already happened.

> Step 4: Incorporate your work from steps 1-3 into a document, usually a narrative that is dated in the future, but written in the present tense.

[20] http://www.inc.com/magazine/20110201/creating-a-company-vision.html

(See the example below from a Medicaid health plan.)

Steps 5 – 6: Continually redraft the initial document.

Step 7: Stamp the vision as draft and circulate for feedback.

Step 8: Share the vision with everyone who will be involved with implementing it or influencing the outcome.

Below is an example of a 2020 vision (abridged) that was created using this process by a Medicaid health plan's maternity care management team:

2020 Vision of Maternity Care

It's December 15, 2020 and we are at a celebration dinner for the extraordinary accomplishments of our Maternity Care effort. We are proud of the results we have achieved together, and are anticipating the time we will be able to spend with family and friends during the well-deserved holiday break.

Here's all of the great stuff that's happening!

Transportation to and from appointments is no longer a barrier to care. Our contract with the transportation company provides members with an easy way to arrange transportation. Members can also pick up free transportation tokens at providers' offices.

Pregnant mothers are happy with their free smart phones and phone service. They are using their phones to schedule appointments, get reminders, and arrange for transportation and babysitting. Additionally, the Community Outreach team and members are using a maternity app for video chats. Homebound members are using their phones and tablets for telemedicine visits.

The phone's maternity apps provide educational information including:
- Dietary and vitamin recommendations
- Access to health risk assessments
- Access to incentive programs
- Reminders about key health milestones
- A way to capture symptoms and issues
- A weight gain calculator
- A tool to help manage stress and negative feelings.

Pregnant moms participating in the care program are grateful to be receiving weekly text messages that provide them with reminders to see their doctor, education about labor signs and symptoms, sleep safety, etc. Members are also pleased that they can earn a $10 gift card just for joining the program, and receive free items including diapers, a Sleep Sack, a pacifier, books, a picture magnet, and even a portable crib!

Multiple services are available in-home. We have a contract for doctors on demand for in-home visits to our pregnant mothers.

We are utilizing home-health technology including fetal monitoring services.

We have a robust pregnant member tracking system. As members are identified as pregnant, we can see how they are progressing during their nine months of pregnancy. The system lets us prioritize members by risk and see who is attending their appointments.

Our systems are fully integrated. We see real-time information on anything happening with a member. This includes members' interactions with our departments such as pharmacy, rapid response, and all of our outside vendors. Our systems pull all data together and show a single view. The integrated systems enable us to efficiently serve the members. We have a stronger bond with the providers because we can have deeper, more informed conversations about the members. We are making proactive recommendations rather than asking what is happening. This makes us unique among health networks.

We have a way to capture the return on investment and the savings we have enabled due to healthy pregnant members and healthy babies. We can show performance improvements from fewer Caesarian sections and neonatal intensive care stays.

We can run our own reports, which provide us with information such as performance trends. We love that we do not have to spend substantial time manually generating reports. We can see, real-time, what appointments a member has attended and whether we are tracking to performance goals.

The above vision example is for a project. A vision can also be applied to an entire company, a department, a division, a small team, a facility, a product, or many other entities. As an individual, if you cannot convince others to create a vision with you, go ahead and start writing one. You may pick up other people along the way, and if you don't, it can serve as your personal vision for a project or how you do your own work.

For More Information: Weinzweig goes into detail on visions in his book, _A Lapsed Anarchist's Approach to Building a Great Business_.

Summarizing unhealthy practice -- Avoiding disengagement:

Avoid traditional preparation of a vision statement where executives go on a retreat to write a short, high-level statement to which most employees doing the front-line work cannot relate. It is a mistake to involve only a small number of executives in creating the vision. While a vision may start with a small group of people, as many people as possible should have the opportunity to comment on and shape the vision.

What you could do to promote engagement:

To promote engagement through visioning, simply start with one or more areas that you influence or manage. Go through the eight steps Ari Weinzweig recommends, and review some of the examples on the Zingermans.com website. You'll get the hang of it with a little practice!

23. Pursue Frontline Quick Wins

"In order to succeed in business and differentiate yourself from competitors, you do not have to be 1000% better at one thing; you have to be 1% better at 1000 things!"

Jan Carlzon

We believe in thinking big – swinging for the fences – to come up with a bold, exciting, motivating vision and design. If you start from scratch and work backwards from where you to be, you can often generate a range of ideas that span various implementation timeframes.

The vision and design provide the inspiration to spark employee engagement. However, to sustain and nurture this engagement, thinking big needs to be accompanied by short-term successes. People need hope and a sense that what they are doing is making a difference, especially in organizations where change efforts have failed repeatedly. If you want employees to continue contributing to an improvement effort, you must continually give them hope. Share with them the progress you're making while working together on bigger impact goals. This is why we like the idea of "thinking big but starting small" with "quick win" projects that bring about one or more implemented changes within a short period – anywhere from same day to six months. As discussed above, the Aquafresh toothpaste example in which line workers were given authority to spend up to $500 on a repair to the production line without having to ask the plant manager for approval, was the quickest of wins and energized the employees' engagement.

One of our colleagues advises against "trying to boil the ocean," meaning that you try to implement so much at once that it is an impossible endeavor. We have personally seen people try to implement a large system-wide change, but fail to accomplish a single goal. One painful software development project dragged on for more than two years, and those called on to give input became disillusioned after not seeing any fruits of their labors. Instead, we have found it effective to keep the vision in mind but start with one or more items that you can implement quickly.

One approach we've found successful for implementing big projects is to create quick wins within a longer-term project by implementing in iterations. For example, we facilitated the design and implementation of a global procurement contracts management system at GlaxoSmithKline (GSK). The first iteration of the system was programmed from scratch and was live within six weeks after user requirements had been defined. The team was able to build the system very quickly because, without losing sight of the big picture, they programmed a single piece of functionality that the users said was very important: contract templates that could be downloaded by procurement professionals for use in contracting with suppliers.

Six weeks later, GSK released functionality that allowed the signed contracts to be uploaded, searched, and viewed.

The users were delighted! It helped tremendously, of course, that they were deeply involved in specifying and designing their ideal system. It also helped that GSK didn't make the users wait for months or longer for perfection. The involvement in design got employees engaged, and the quick, repeated delivery of improvements won them over.

Achieving quick wins also gets senior executives on board by delivering benefits they can point to. Commenting on the GSK contracts system, one vice president said, "I've never seen a system implementation go so smoothly and with no complaining."

We have also found that user engagement can be sustained by implementing some quick-win projects alongside some longer-term ones with a six-month to two-year timeframe. The fruits of the short-term projects sustain confidence in the longer-term projects and in the people involved.

We sometimes use the following diagram to communicate a think-big-but-start-small project approach:

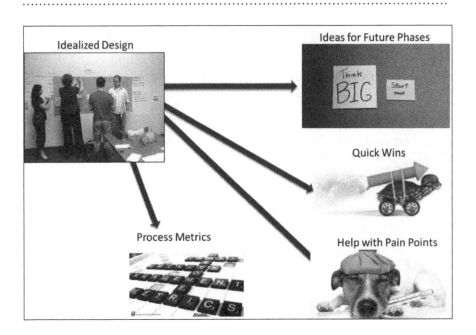

Summarizing unhealthy practice -- Avoiding disengagement:

Stakeholders are likely to become disengaged, resistant, or even hostile to your grand vision for change if they must wait a long time for you to articulate it or if the vision provides only long-term solutions without any quick wins along the way. They are also less likely to want to participate in future change projects.

What you could do to promote engagement:

After you've identified your ideal design and your vision, start your implementation with several quick-win projects. Celebrating those quick wins brings two benefits. First, people who have been involved will feel appreciated, and it will further energize them. Second, those who haven't been involved will see that exciting progress is being made and that involvement results in benefits to those who participate. Some will get involved because they don't want to be left out.

Start with quick-win projects that have a good chance of success and are not overly expensive or complicated to implement. Quick wins provide credibility for management and hope, faith, and courage for employees to next take on bigger projects. Make sure to leave time and resources to incorporate additional user ideas once people have a chance to use the solutions.

Part VIII

More Heads are Better than One

24. Use the Influence of a Group

It is difficult to feel engaged when it seems we are getting little or nothing accomplished. Unfortunately, this situation develops in many large organizations when departments, groups, teams, and individuals push their own agendas. Paralysis results because people are working at cross purposes.

Fortunately, there are powerful ways to get things moving. For example, we can learn from Ben Franklin about getting ideas implemented. In addition to his many accomplishments in science, inventions, and government, Ben Franklin cofounded a number of community institutions: the first volunteer fire company in Philadelphia; the first public library in the American colonies; the first hospital in the American colonies; and, an educational academy that became one of the first universities in the American colonies. Note that we said that Franklin "cofounded" these institutions. In his autobiography, Franklin shared a fascinating insight about how he was able to get things done. He realized that when he presented an idea as his own, he had less success convincing others to go along than when the ideas were presented as coming from a group of people.

Here's how Franklin learned this. He had formed a group he called a "Junto" that would meet regularly to discuss the ideas of the day. Once, when he met with another group to seek support for a proposal, he mentioned that the proposal had come from the Junto. He discovered that, when presented that way, others were more willing to support the idea.

One of our early personal experiences is consistent with Franklin's observation of the power of group ideas. In one improvement project, we spent a Saturday with 48 stakeholders from the Academy of Vocal Arts, a premier opera training school based in Center City Philadelphia. Faculty, students, management, board members, and benefactors used idealized design to design their ideal opera school from scratch. Their resulting design included an expanded facility, outdoor public performances in the summer, performing around the world to attract the best students, full scholarships for all, and so on.

The story of the stakeholders' ideal facility is inspiring. They envisioned that it would include a recording studio, a performance theater, sound-proof practice rooms, and ample space for building stage scenery. Near the end of the initial idealized design session, all 48 people agreed that to realize their vision for the facility they should buy the building next door. Once a plan was developed, they sought financial support from one of the benefactors who had been involved in the session. She asked, "How much will the project cost?" When they said "$3.5 million," she quickly replied, "I'll pay for the entire thing." (!) The building was purchased and renovated, doubling the facility's size. Two years later, we had a conversation with the executive director. He reflected on the power of the group process with all 48 stakeholders: "The idea for buying the building next door was not new; I had previously discussed it with a couple of board members. But the idea went nowhere. Only when we got the whole group together did we get the energy, commitment, and alignment to make it happen."

In a second experience involving the power of group ideas, we found credibility to be another factor that built support. In a project for the director of travel at a Fortune 100 company, we ran customer idealized design sessions with employees who were heavy travelers. We had also invited the account executives from major airline, car rental, travel booking and credit card suppliers. The employees designed their ideal corporate travel process, offering numerous ideas. Months after the sessions, after several ideas had been implemented, the travel director told us that her credibility with the suppliers was much higher because they realized that when she advocated for an idea, she was not speaking for just herself but on behalf of a group of people. Furthermore, she believed that implementation had been so successful because of the group process.

Summarizing unhealthy practice -- Avoiding disengagement:

Think about times when an individual needs to dominate an idea by having it be theirs, by imposing it on others, or by not being open to suggestions. More often than not, others do not support it or at least passively resist it. Worse, they may actively undermine it. Don't try to go it alone so you can get all the glory. Trying to be the hero and save the day with your own ideas is not likely to satisfy anyone in the long run, especially you.

What you could do to promote engagement:

When a group owns an idea, it gains support and lift. Create an environment where groups are encouraged to offer ideas and participate in selecting the ones that garner the most energy. If you have an idea, try to hold off on pushing others to accept it. We have often found it effective to get a dialogue going about what could be done, and wait a while before offering your idea. It's possible that your idea will be adopted, but it is also possible that better ideas will emerge.

Ultimately, when a group is able to jointly own an implementation, this translates to engagement because the group "owns" that impact.

25. Assume You Are Wrong

"How does humility manifest itself in leadership and in life? A humble person is more concerned about what is right than about being right, about acting on good ideas than having the ideas, about embracing new truth than defending an outdated position, about building the team than exalting self, about recognizing contribution than being recognized for making it."

Stephen M.R. Covey

When we were starting our careers, we had lots of ideas we wanted to try out in the world. We were eager to share our ideas about what would work. However, we didn't understand how important it is to first build relationships and trust before people will be open to another's ideas.

We once had an opportunity to do a pro bono project with an elementary school in a disadvantaged neighborhood. We thought it was a great opportunity to try out our ideas. Fortunately, we didn't have that chance. We had brought along a community development genius named Herman Wrice. When we arrived, we were met by the principal, a couple of teachers, and about 15 mothers from the parent and teacher organization. After they thanked us for coming, the mothers began talking about how they wanted to hold a community fair and fundraiser in the school's playground. They wanted to create better connections between the school and the community while raising money to support the teachers' programs. They painted a picture for us: tables of baked goods for sale, games such as bean bag toss, a water dunking tank, face painting, a hot dog stand, and so on. Herman jumped on the idea, saying it was fabulous and that we were fully supportive. Fast forward four months, and the fair was held on a beautiful spring day. It was a huge success, and it raised more than $2,000 to support the teachers.

After the success of the project that had been defined by the stakeholders, we had established huge trust and a great relationship. We could then offer our ideas on what would help the community. Many of these were accepted without resistance.

We can imagine how much harder it would have been if we had pushed our own ideas from the very start. We translated our learnings from the school experience to efforts to engage employees, and found that the lesson of assuming you are wrong about what is needed holds in corporations as well. We found that if organizations and/or managers give employees a voice in the future of the department, process, product, system, or service, and a chance to be involved in creating it, they are much more engaged than if a decision was made without their input.

We have also seen employee disengagement and lack of support when senior executives, or the external consultants they bring in, develop their own strategies and plans instead of listening to their subordinates, the people doing the actual work of the business. Solutions devised with little or no input from the effected employees are usually not well supported and often fail.

We've witnessed frustrating examples of failure up close. In one example of executive failure, leadership put in place inadequate schedules for delivering an IT system project. Middle management and frontline staff were not consulted on the timelines, and there was fear of consequences of missing the deadlines. The employees responsible for delivery of the system did not have sufficient time to gather business and user requirements. Their morale plummeted because they knew that what was being delivered could have been so much better. The IT system was put in place but not used, and the user-focused workers tried to push for improvements. However, a new, tight deadline for a second wave of functionality was looming so the IT resources were not available to make the needed fixes for the first wave, even though the system did not satisfy the users' needs. The project team was extremely frustrated because they saw failure about to repeat itself. Because of the rush, many design decisions were made centrally, and users were not engaged as fully as they should have been.

What you could do to promote engagement:
What should these executives have done, and what are the learnings you could apply? We believe that the single most important missing attribute in these examples and in many such instances is trust in the project team and frontline users/customers. Leaders should have recognized that creating something great takes a lot longer than one might think. Instead of pushing an executive strategy or saying "Get everything done fast," they should have trusted the project team and frontline staff to set the pace and decide what should be done first. We are big believers in the

approach of "Think big but start small." This allows people to start with what the users say is most valuable, and deliver something that works, leading to user engagement in defining and delivering the next set of functionality.

By the way, you don't have to be an executive for the "assume you're wrong" rule to apply. As mentioned in other chapters, you can listen closely to your internal or external customers and involve them in designing solutions. You can get a high level of participation in input on requirements and then have a smaller team regularly reach back to the users for feedback as they complete the design and implement the solutions.

A Call to Action

"If we could change ourselves, the tendencies in the world would also change. As a man changes his own nature, so does the attitude of the world change towards him ... We need not wait to see what others do."

Mahatma Gandhi

"The secret of getting ahead is getting started. The secret of getting started is breaking your complex overwhelming tasks into small manageable tasks, and starting on the first one."

Mark Twain

Our long-time friend and colleague, Gregg Brandyberry, puts it in simple terms: "Let's not play small ball." He has supported putting into practice many of the ideas in this book. The environments he has created inside companies have been joyful places for employees. The joyfulness derives from making a difference in the world, feeling part of something special, being challenged, providing extraordinary service, being part of a we're-great-together culture, feeling appreciated, and having positive human connections.

As we described at the outset of this book, most people are disengaged, to varying degrees, from their organizations. However, it doesn't have to be that way. We wrote this book to share approaches that you can put into practice, many very easily and with little or no cost. YOU can make the difference! You can select the approaches you believe will work best in your situation. And, since the approaches interact with each other to produce more effect, the more you do the better. It's like growing a vegetable garden. Factors such as soil quality, sunlight, temperature, and water interact synergistically. The more you get right, the better the bounty.

It's encouraging that there are things YOU can do to get employees and users engaged, no matter where you are in an organization. We're reminded of a story Russell Ackoff used to tell. He was running a management education course for executives of a big American auto company. Vice presidents were the first management level to go through the course. When the course concluded, the VPs said, "Russ, the ideas you presented are great, but we cannot implement them without the support of the senior vice presidents. You should be talking with them." Russ replied that the SVPs would be the next group participating in the course. And, do you know what the SVPs said at the end of their course? They said, "Russ, the ideas you presented are great, but we cannot implement them without the support of the CEO. You should be talking with him." Russ responded that the CEO would be the next person participating in the course. At the end of the course, the CEO said to Russ, "The ideas you presented are great, but I cannot implement them without the support of my subordinates."

Ackoff's point was the best place to start is wherever you are. We agree with him. Start with what affects your area. And remember, it's easier to seek forgiveness than permission. To seek permission is to seek denial.

We have been able to apply all of the ideas in this book by starting within the areas we've managed. More often than not, the practices have spread beyond our areas once others saw the successes. Have we sometimes run into opposition or failed? Absolutely. But when we failed, we picked up the pieces, learned from it, and went on to do better things and to bigger opportunities. Isn't it better to feel alive than to play it safe? Playing it safe is no longer safe, if it ever really was. In a rapidly changing world, standing still and trying to hold onto the past are more risky than doing nothing.

So, get out there and think big, even if you start small!

About the Author

Jason Magidson helps organizations create extraordinary engagement, transformation, and innovation that serves customers, employees, suppliers, and community.

Jason has authored two other books – *Idealized Design: Dissolving Tomorrow's Crisis Today* (co-authored with Russell L. Ackoff and Herb Addison) – and *Laughter is the Salt of Life: People's True Stories of the Hardest They've Ever Laughed.* Jason has also written articles for *Harvard Business Review*, the *Journal of Product Innovation Management*, and the *Journal of Business Strategy*.

Jason has helped companies including IKEA, GlaxoSmithKline, Anheuser-Busch, Merck, AmeriHealth Caritas, DuPont, SAP, and Jones Lang LaSalle with transformation and user/employee engagement. Jason's projects have included software development, R&D, manufacturing, sales, procurement, finance, new market development, risk management, medical care management, human resources, and legal, among others.

Jason was a cofounder and board chair of Adopt a Neighborhood for Development. He currently serves on the board of trustees of Philadelphia Free School.

Jason received a B.S. from The Wharton School of the University of Pennsylvania and a Ph.D. from Union Institute & University in systems thinking and interactive management. His doctoral thesis focused on involving users in the design of products, services, and systems.

Jason, his wife, and their three daughters live in the Philadelphia area.